O9-ABI-746

Poison Ivy

This weed (above) causes an itchy rash if you touch it. Poison ivy grows as a vine or shrub. Try to remember what the leaves look like, and do not touch them or other parts of the plant. If you do touch poison ivy, washing your hands as soon as possible may reduce the itching. Your local drugstore will have various remedies that will help.

Butterfly Flight Periods

The flight period of a butterfly species is the time of year when you are most likely to see the adult of that species. Butterflies of some species have one generation of young per year and their young emerge at about the same time every year—this species would be said to have one brood per year. In other species, young butterflies emerge from two or more broods born to a species per year. The months listed after the number of broods represents the full length of the flight period throughout the range.

Flight periods may vary from region to region depending on climate and when food plants are available. Therefore, a butterfly such as the whirlabout (see page 16) has a continuous flight period in warm southern regions, meaning new young are always emerging in these areas and one may always spot a whirlabout there. But, in cooler regions in the North the species has two broods per season and may be seen sometime between the months of April and September.

World Book's

SCIENCE & NATURE GUIDES

BUTTERFLIES

OF THE UNITED STATES AND CANADA

World Book, Inc.
a Scott Fetzer company
Chicago

Scientific names

In this book, after the common name of an organism (life form) is given, that organism's scientific name usually appears. Scientific names are put into a special type of lettering, called italic, *which looks like this.*

The first name in a scientific name is the genus. A genus consists of very similar groups, but the members of these different groups usually cannot breed with one another. The second name given is the species. Every known organism belongs to a particular species. Members of a species can breed with one another, and the young grow up to look very much like the parents.

An animal's scientific name is the same worldwide. This helps scientists and students to know which animal is being discussed, since the animal may have many different common names. When you see a name like *Danaus plexippus*, you know that the genus is *Danaus* and the species is *plexippus*. *Danaus plexippus* is the scientific name for the monarch butterfly (see page 17).

Butterfly-hunter's Code

1 **Always go collecting with a friend,** and always tell an adult where you are going.

2 **Treat all butterflies with care**—they are delicate creatures and can easily be injured or killed by rough handling.

3 **Ask permission** before exploring or crossing private property.

4 **Keep to existing roads, trails, and pathways** wherever possible.

5 **Keep away from crops and leave fence gates** as you find them.

6 **Wear long pants, shoes, a hat, and a long-sleeved shirt** in tick country.

7 **Take your litter home.**

This edition published in the United States of America by World Book, Inc., Chicago.

WORLD BOOK and the GLOBE DEVICE are registered trademarks or trademarks of World Book, Inc.

World Book, Inc.
233 North Michigan Avenue
Chicago, IL 60601 USA

For information about other World Book publications, visit our Web site **http://www.worldbook.com,** or call **1-800-WORLDBK (967-5325).** For information about sales to schools and libraries, call **1-800-975-3250 (United States); 1-800-837-5365 (Canada).**

Copyright © 2005 Chrysalis Children's Book Group, an imprint of Chrysalis Books Group Plc
The Chrysalis Building, Bramley Road, London, W10 6SP
www.chrysalis.com

Library of Congress Cataloging-in-Publication Data

Butterflies of the United States and Canada.
        p. cm. — (World Book's science & nature guides)
    Includes bibliographical references (p.).
    ISBN 0-7166-4211-5 — ISBN 0-7166-4208-5 (set)
    1. Butterflies—North America—Juvenile literature. 2. Butterflies—North America—Identification—Juvenile literature. I. World Book, Inc. II. Series.

QL548 .B88 2005
595.7'89'097—dc22
                                                                2004043485

Text and captions based on *Butterflies of North America* by John Feltwell.

Habitat paintings by Philip Weare; headbands by Antonia Phillips; identification and activities illustrations by Mr. Gay Galsworthy.

For World Book:
General Managing Editor: Paul A. Kobasa
Editorial: Shawn Brennan, Maureen Liebenson, Christine Sullivan
Research: Madolynn Cronk, Lynn Durbin, Cheryl Graham, Karen McCormack, Loranne Shields, Hilary Zawidowski
Librarian: Jon Fjortoft
Permissions: Janet Peterson
Graphics and Design: Sandra Dyrlund, Anne Fritzinger
Indexing: Aamir Burki, David Pofelski
Pre-press and Manufacturing: Carma Fazio, Steve Hueppchen, Jared Svoboda, Madelyn Underwood
Text Processing: Curley Hunter, Gwendolyn Johnson
Proofreading: Anne Dillon

Printed in China
1 2 3 4 5 6 7 8 9 10 09 08 07 06 05 04

Contents

**Introduction To
    Butterflies** **4–7**
What To Look For 6–7

**Found Almost
    Everywhere** **8–17**
A Butterfly Safari 18–19

**Bogs &
    Other Wetlands** **20–29**
Butterflies To Be 30–31

**Meadows &
    Grasslands** **32–51**
Raising Butterflies 42–43
Butterfly Garden 52–53

Deserts & Mountains . . **54–61**
Keeping Records 62–63

**Woodlands
& Clearings** **64–77**

Find Out More 78
Index &
    Additional Resources 79–81

Entries *like this*
indicate pages
featuring projects
you can do!

Introduction To Butterflies

Fluttering butterflies live everywhere in the United States and Canada. You can spot them in a variety of places—on mountains, in damp bogs, in sunny woodlands, flying above the desert, and in your own yard. Not only are they beautiful to look at, but they also have a fascinating life cycle. This book will help you to become a butterfly spotter. It shows the butterflies you are most likely to see, in the habitat, or type of countryside, where you are most likely to see them, and this will help you in learning to identify them. Where butterflies choose to live depends on the flowers and plants on which they like to feed. So knowing a butterfly's favorite plant, and where that plant grows, is a great help in knowing where to spot that butterfly.

The life of a butterfly

Butterflies go through four very different stages in their lives. The first stage is the egg. From the egg hatches a larva, called a caterpillar. The caterpillar eventually enters a pupal phase, in which it forms a chrysalis. Finally, from the chrysalis emerges an adult butterfly. When insects change from one form to another like this, it is called complete metamorphosis (change in form), because each stage is completely different from the one before.

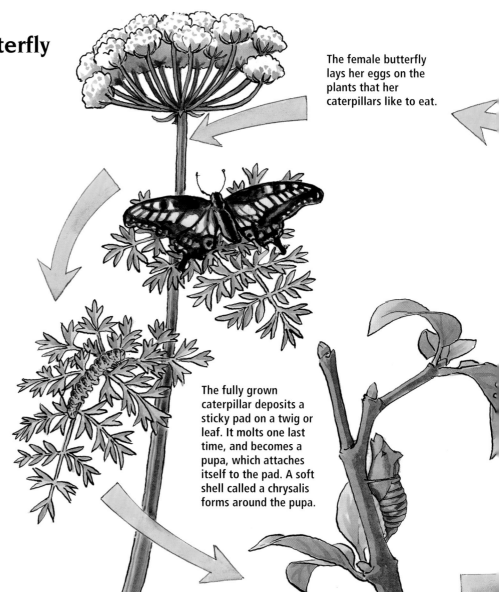

The female butterfly lays her eggs on the plants that her caterpillars like to eat.

The caterpillar hatches (it eats its way out of the egg that encloses it) and immediately starts to feed on the plant. As it grows larger, it has to molt (shed its skin), because caterpillar skin does not stretch.

The fully grown caterpillar deposits a sticky pad on a twig or leaf. It molts one last time, and becomes a pupa, which attaches itself to the pad. A soft shell called a chrysalis forms around the pupa.

How to use this book

To identify a butterfly you don't recognize, like the two shown here, follow these steps.

1 **Draw a quick sketch of the butterfly** (see page 19) in your field notebook. Draw the outline first, then fill in any other features you notice. Write down where and when you spotted the butterfly.

2 **Determine what habitat you are in.** If you read the descriptions at the start of each section, you'll soon see which one matches your location. Each habitat has a different picture band.

3 **Look through the section covering that habitat.** The picture and information given for each butterfly will help you identify it. The brightly patterned butterfly shown to the right is a tiger swallowtail (see page 17).

4 **If you can't find the butterfly there,** look through the other sections. Some butterflies can live in several different habitats.

5 **Sometimes, the females look different than the males,** like this cloudless sulfur (see right and page 16). Make sure you study the pictures and the text carefully. **The male (♂) and female (♀) wings are shown for each species.**

6 **What month is it?** Many butterflies are seen only at certain times of the year. See the fact caption for the flight period of each butterfly.

7 **If you still can't find the butterfly,** you may have to look in a larger field guide. You may have seen a very rare butterfly! Or it might be a moth (see page 53).

When the adult inside the chrysalis is fully formed, the chrysalis splits open and a wet butterfly crawls out. The butterfly spreads its wings, lets them dry, and then flies off in search of nectar.

Habitat Picture Bands

This book is divided into different habitats (or types of countryside). Each habitat has a different picture band at the top of the page. These are shown below.

Found Almost Everywhere

Bogs & Other Wetlands

Meadows & Grasslands

Deserts & Mountains

Woodlands & Clearings

What To Look For

Parts of a butterfly

Like all insects, a typical adult butterfly has three sections to its body and three pairs of legs. The three body sections are the head, the thorax, and the abdomen.

Each butterfly has two pairs of wings: two forewings and two hindwings. The wings are covered in scales, which give them their color. When you are trying to identify a butterfly, take note of the following:

- Is it large or small?
- What color and shape are its wings?
- Do they have patterns on them?
- Don't forget to look at the underside of the wings, as the color and patterns there may be completely different.
- What are the antennae like?

The head of a butterfly has a pair of antennae, which are club-shaped at the tip, and a pair of big eyes, called compound eyes.

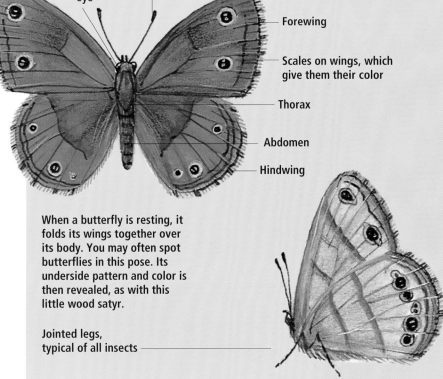

Compound eye

Antenna with club at the tip

Forewing

Scales on wings, which give them their color

Thorax

Abdomen

Hindwing

When a butterfly is resting, it folds its wings together over its body. You may often spot butterflies in this pose. Its underside pattern and color is then revealed, as with this little wood satyr.

Jointed legs, typical of all insects

Wing shapes

The wing shapes of butterflies vary from rounded to triangular to long and thin. Some wings have "tails" on them; others have wavy edges.

The gray skipper's wings are triangular in shape.

The white admiral's hindwings have wavy edges.

The clouded skipper's wings are pointed.

The zebra swallowtail has a long tail on each of its hindwings.

Antennae

Looking at butterflies' antennae is a useful way to identify them, as antennae vary from type to type.

The swarthy skipper, like all skippers, has hooked antennae.

The parnassian's antennae are striped.

Important Families of Butterflies

Color and markings

The color and markings (patterns) on a butterfly's wings are one of the first things you'll notice.

The American swallowtail has orange and black marks on its hindwings called "eyespots." These look like big eyes and frighten away would-be predators.

Male butterflies often have a black mark near the top of the forewing, like the one on this saltgrass skipper.

The purple bog fritillary has a very noticeable pattern of black dots, dashes, and crescents against an orange background.

Swallowtails

These butterflies are quite large and are lively fliers. The "true" swallowtails are all brightly colored and have taillike extensions on their hindwings. One group of swallowtails, the parnassians are smaller and have no extensions on their hindwings. A typical parnassian is the clodius parnassian, also known as the American apollo.

Whites and sulfurs

Butterflies in this group are medium-sized and are often white or yellow. Some of them have bright orange tips to their wings. Males and females often look completely different from one another, as does this wolf-face sulfur.

Skippers

These include the smallest of all butterflies; they are also the most numerous in North America. The name "skipper" comes from the way that they fly—with a rapid, skipping movement. Like this greenish little skipper, they have very distinctive hooked antennae, very hairy bodies, and triangular wings.

Brush-footed butterflies

This is a very large family of usually medium-sized butterflies. Unlike other families, this group has short, weak forelegs, called *brush feet*, which contain special organs to help locate food. Brush-footed butterflies are usually fast fliers. They include the browns, which are usually some shade of brown, the milkweeds, and the snouts, which have very noticeable beaklike mouth parts— such as this southern snout butterfly.

Blues, coppers, hairstreaks, harvesters, and metalmarks

These butterflies are usually small and colorful, and they like wild flowers. Blues, like this spring azure, are usually blue; the coppers are usually copper-colored, and the hairstreaks usually have tails. The harvesters are bigger and do not visit flowers. Metalmarks, like this Mormon metalmark, get their name from the shiny, metallic markings on their wings that glint in the sunshine.

Found Almost Everywhere

Some butterflies feed on very common plants like clover, and these are the butterflies you are most likely to see without too much hunting. You also may see the butterflies from this section in the other habitats covered in this book—grasslands, deserts, mountains, woodlands, clearings, bogs, and wetlands. Butterflies shown in other sections may live in other types of landscapes as well.

Roadside habitats are exactly that—grassy areas at the sides of roads. These are good places to spot butterflies, as there are often wild flowers growing there for the butterflies to visit. Next time you go for a drive, even along a highway, look for butterflies on the grassy edges. Parks and yards are also ideal places to spot butterflies. They are filled with colorful flowers just perfect for sipping nectar, and leaves just waiting to be nibbled on by hungry caterpillars. A habitat that would seem more unlikely is waste ground, but it is often home to many types of butterflies. Waste ground includes railroad yards or vacant lots; these lands often have fast-growing weeds and hardy wild flowers growing through cracks in the concrete. The butterflies feed on very familiar plants, such as clover, milkweed, and daisies. This picture shows butterflies covered in this section—how many can you recognize?

Clockwise from the top left: pipevine swallowtail, giant swallowtail, orange sulfur, monarch, gray hairstreak, spring azure, tawny-edged skipper, and a brown elfin in the center.

Found Almost Everywhere

Silver-studded Blue
(Plebejus acmon)

Also called the acmon blue. Males of this species have lilac-blue wings, while females' wings are mostly brown. Both males and females have a row of bright orange spots along the edges of their hindwings. They have pale gray undersides with black dots, which also feature orange spots on the hindwings. Fringes on the edges of the wings are white. These butterflies can be seen fluttering close to the ground searching for flowers in many different habitats. Its caterpillars feed on wild buckwheat, locoweed, trefoils, deer weed, lupines, and knotwood. The species is found in southwestern Canada and the western United States.

Family: Lycaenidae—Wingspan: ¾–1⅛ in (2–2.8 cm)
Flight period: Continuous, from March to October

Small Apollo
(Parnassius phoebus)

This butterfly is also known as the small parnassian. Males of this type of butterfly are cream-colored with red spots on the hindwings; females are darker and their wings have transparent areas. Both males and females have black-and-gray markings on forewings and hindwings. If you can get close enough, you will notice that they have black-and-white stripes on their antennae. The small apollo flies around flowered areas like meadows. The caterpillars are black with yellow spots and feed on sedums. The species is found from Alaska through western Canada to southern California and in the Rocky Mountains.

Family: Papilionidae
Wingspan: 2¼–3 in (5.5–7.5 cm)
Flight period: One, from May to August

Cabbage Butterfly
(Pieris rapae)

Also known as the small white, this butterfly is milky-white on top and greenish-yellow underneath. You can tell the males from the females easily—males have one black spot on each forewing, while females have two. This butterfly flies in all sorts of habitats, from backyards to fields, from cities to foothills. A very common butterfly, most gardeners know it well. They see it as a pest, because cabbage butterfly caterpillars, true to their name, nibble away on cabbage plants, as well as other plants in the mustard family, such as broccoli and radishes. The caterpillars are bright green with yellow stripes. The species is found in all of the United States and southern Canada.

Family: Pieridae—Wingspan: 1¾–2¼ in (4.5–5.5 cm)
Flight period: Many, from March to November

Eastern Tailed Blue
(Everes comyntas)

So-called because of its hindwing tail, the male butterfly has violet-blue wings with little black, and sometimes orange, dots on the hindwing. In the female the wings are usually brown, but may show the same markings as the male. The underside of the wing for both males and females is grayish-white with black spots and orange spots near the tail. A white fringe runs all around the wings. Look for this butterfly fluttering close to the ground on roadsides and in fields, backyards, and farmland areas. The caterpillars feed on clovers, beans, and trefoils. The species is found in the eastern half of the United States, and, occasionally, on the West Coast.

Family: Lycaenidae
Wingspan: ¾–1 in (2–2.5 cm)
Flight period: Several flights, between spring and fall

Western Swallowtail
(Papilio zelicaon)

Also known as the anise swallowtail, this butterfly has thick black borders framing its wings. There are large yellow markings on both forewings and hindwings. Blue marks and orange eyespots appear on the hindwings. Females of this type of butterfly are bigger than the males. They fly in many areas, from forest clearings to city streets, from mountain tops to canyons. The caterpillars have green-and-black bands with orange spots. They like to eat young leaves and buds of such plants as fennel, cow parsnip, carrots, and parsley. It is found in the western United States and southwestern Canada.

Family: Papilionidae—Wingspan: 2¾–3 in (7–7.5 cm)
Flight period: One in the North;
all year around in the Southwest

Mourning Cloak
(Nymphalis antiopa)

This big butterfly is hard to miss, with its yellow border and row of blue spots against a maroon background. The underside of the wings is dark, which is good for camouflage. You will see this butterfly in many different habitats, from forest edges to open woodlands, from yards and parks to towns. The caterpillars, black and bristly with white speckles, feed in groups on willow, elm, hackberry, and cottonwood. This species is found in most of the United States and Canada, except in the Arctic region.

Family: Nymphalidae—Wingspan: 3–3½ in (7.5–9 cm)
Flight period: Continuous

Pipevine Swallowtail
(Battus philenor)

You can recognize this butterfly by the dark gray to black forewings and the greenish color on the hindwings. The underside of its hindwings reveals a flash of big, bright orange spots. Look for the pipevine swallowtail fluttering by such yard plants as azalea, buddleia, and honeysuckle. The black and orange-spotted caterpillars hatched by this species eat plants that cause them to taste nasty, so predators, such as birds, know to keep well away.

Family: Papilionidae
Wingspan: 2¾–3½ in
(7–9 cm)
Flight period: Two to three,
from January to October

Greenish Little Skipper
(Amblyscirtes hegon)

Also known as the pepper and salt skipper, this butterfly has greenish-brown wings, which have a brassy shine. Fringes at the edges of the wings are checkered. You can spot this butterfly resting on rocks in the stony canyons and rocky slopes of mountain ranges, by roadsides, and in woodlands. It is found in the southwest of the United States.
Family: Hesperiidae
Wingspan: 1–1¼ in (2.5–3 cm)
Flight period: One from May to August

♂♀

Saltgrass Skipper
(Polites sabuleti)

♂♀   ♂

Also called the sandhill skipper, this butterfly is a rich brown with black-and-orange marks. Males, which are smaller than females, have a black mark on the forewing. The underside of the wings is lighter, with yellow veins. The saltgrass skipper likes to fly around sand dunes on the coast, as well as in grassy areas, such as city backyards. The caterpillars feed on grasses. This species is found on the west coast from British Columbia to Mexico and as far inland as Colorado.
Family: Hesperiidae—Wingspan: ¾–1¼ in (2–3 cm)
Flight period: One in higher elevations and several in lower regions, from March to October

Giant Swallowtail
(Papilio cresphontes)

Citrus growers see the giant swallowtail as a pest. It lays its eggs on citrus trees, and its brown or olive caterpillars feed on those trees. The caterpillars are called orange dogs. The giant swallowtail may be found along roadsides or woodland glades. Very large and mostly brown, this butterfly has two broad bands of yellow spots crossing the wings, and orange spots at the base of the hindwings. The underside of the wings is pale yellow. The females are much larger than the males. The species is found on the East Coast of the United States, west to the Mississippi River.
Family: Papilionidae
Wingspan: 3½–5½ in (9–14 cm)
Flight period: Continuous in the South, late spring and summer in the North

Tawny-edged Skipper
(Polites themistocles)

♂♀

This butterfly is so called because it has bright tawny-gold patches on the edges of both forewings. This contrasts with the dark brown color of the rest of the wings. Males have a dark mark on the forewings, and females have yellow spots. The underside of the wings is lighter in color. You will find this butterfly in grassy areas, including backyards. The caterpillars, which can be either maroon or tan, feed on different types of grasses. This species is found in most of southern Canada and the northern United States, but it is rare in the Northwest.
Family: Hesperiidae
Wingspan: ¾–1 in (2–2.5 cm)
Flight period: One from June to August in northern areas, two from April to September in the South

♂♀

Common Checkered Skipper
(Pyrgus communis)

As its name suggests, this butterfly has a checkered pattern on its black-and-white wings. You can tell males from females because they are more strongly patterned. The wings are similar in pattern underneath, but feature an off-white band. The checkered skipper flies in many habitats, including foothills, parks, backyards, roadsides, and riverbanks. Its caterpillars feed on mallows. This species is found in most of the United States into southern Canada.
Family: Hesperiidae
Wingspan: ¾–1¼ in (2–3 cm)
Flight period: Numerous, all year round in Texas

American Swallowtail
(Papilio polyxenes)

Also known as the black swallowtail, this butterfly has a row of yellow spots and a yellow band across its black wings, with an orange-red eyespot on each hindwing. There is also a scattering of blue across the hindwings—this is stronger in the females of the species. The underside of the wings also has spots, which may be yellow or orange. These butterflies like to fly around open spaces, such as backyards, meadows, and farmland. Parsley or carrot plants will attract them to your backyard. The caterpillars—colored white or green with black bands—feed on Queen Anne's lace (also called wild carrot), cultivated carrot plants, and citrus plants. This species is found in the United States east of the Rocky Mountains and in southeastern Canada.
Family: Papilionidae
Wingspan: 2¾–3½ in (7–9 cm)
Flight period: Three, from February to November

Common Sooty Wing
(Pholisora catullus)

Also known as the roadside rambler, this little butterfly has long, rounded wings, which are black or dark brown. There are crescent-shaped white spots running down each forewing. You will find this butterfly in many habitats, from waste ground and weedy areas in cities to small mountains. Its caterpillars, which are pale green with a dark head, feed on plants such as pigweed, cheeseweed, and lamb's quarters. The species is found in most of the United States.
Family: Hesperiidae
Wingspan: 1–1¼ in (2.5–3 cm)
Flight period: Two, from May to August in the North, March to November in the South

Gray Skipper
(Lerodea eufala)

The gray skipper, also known as the eufala skipper, is quite a plain butterfly, with little pattern. It has triangular wings that are a gray-brown in color. There are some small white spots on the forewings. The underside of the forewing is tan, and the hindwing is brown with gray "dusting." You'll find this butterfly in many habitats, from pine woods to desert valleys, from coasts to roadsides. The caterpillars are bright green with yellow patches and feed on grasses. This species is found in the South and Midwest of the United States.
Family: Hesperiidae
Wingspan: 1–1¼ in (2.5–3 cm)
Flight period: One during early spring in the North; two or more in the South from February to December

Mormon Metalmark
(Apodemia mormo)

Brightly patterned with white spots and black markings against shades of brown and orange, this butterfly should be easy to spot. It flies swiftly and basks in the sunshine in many habitats, from beaches to mountains and deserts. The dark gray caterpillars feed on different kinds of buckwheats. This species is found along the entire West Coast of the United States.

Family: Riodinidae
Wingspan: ¾–1¼ in (2–3 cm)
Flight period: One to two, from March to October

Brown Elfin
(Callophrys augustus)

This very common butterfly has warm-brown wings, with an orange tinge in the females—the underside of the wings is light brown. The males have a black mark on their forewings. The brown elfin flies in woodland glades, chaparral, deserts, and shrubby forests. Its yellowish-green caterpillars feed on many plants, including blueberries, bearberry, azalea, dodder, lilac, and apples. This species is widespread in Canada, the northern United States, and mountainous areas of the eastern and western United States.

Family: Lycaenidae
Wingspan: ¾–1⅛ in (2–2.8 cm)
Flight period: One, from March to June

Gray Hairstreak
(Strymon melinus)

Also known as the common hairstreak, the wings of this butterfly are a rich gray-brown with orange spots on the bottom of the hindwings. Each hindwing has two tails, one long and one short. The underside of the wings is light gray with an orange-and-white line across them and orange patches on the hindwings. This butterfly can be found in many places, from woodlands to coastlines, from parks to roadsides. The green caterpillars feed on corn, oak, cotton, strawberry, and mint. The species is found everywhere in the United States and across southern Canada.

Family: Lycaenidae
Wingspan: 1–1¼ in (2.5–3 cm)
Flight period: Two in the North to three in the South, from April to October

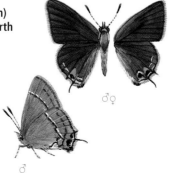

Banded Hairstreak
(Satyrium calanus)

Both males and females have brownish-black wings, but females are more gray. The hindwings have two tails each, one long and one short. Underneath, the wings are crossed by two rows of lines, with orange marks at the base of the hindwings. The banded hairstreak sips nectar from such plants as milkweed, dogbane, and sumac. They live in land along roads, and in forests, parks, and backyards. The yellow-green or brownish caterpillars feed on walnuts, hickories, and oaks. The species is found in southeastern Canada and most of the central and eastern United States.

Family: Lycaenidae
Wingspan: 1–1¼ in (2.5–3 cm)
Flight period: One from June to July

Painted Lady
(Vanessa cardui)

Orange, black, white, and brown marks cover the painted lady's wings; the tips of the forewings are mainly black with white spots. The underside of the hindwings has four blue spots on an olive-green background. This butterfly is not fussy about its habitat, it flies just about anywhere, especially in heavily flowered areas. The caterpillars, purplish and spiny, like to eat thistles. This species is found in most of the United States, northward into Canada as far as the Arctic Circle.

Family: Nymphalidae—Wingspan: About 2–2¾ in (5–7 cm)
Flight period: Continuous in the South, April to October in the North

Spring Azure
(Celastrina argiolus)

This butterfly has sky-blue wings, with brown borders in the female. The underside of the wings is slate-gray with a black checkered border and black spots on the hindwings. As its name suggests, this butterfly is very common in the early spring—when you see it, you know that spring has arrived. The spring azure flies in many types of habitats, from woodlands and roadsides to mountains, clearings, and glades. The caterpillars feed on many types of flowers, including dogwoods, viburnum, and meadowsweets. This species is found in most of Canada and in the United States as far north as Alaska.

Family: Lycaenidae
Wingspan: ¾–1¼ in (2–3 cm)
Flight period: Between one and several from March to August

Red Admiral
(Vanessa atalanta)

This butterfly has bright red bars crossing its forewings. The top of the forewings is black and spotted with white. The hindwings have orange bars on their borders. The underside of the wings has a mottled pattern with black, brown, and blue. The red admiral flies in all sorts of areas, from flowery meadows to rivers and shorelines, from forest clearings to cities. The caterpillars, spiny and patterned with brown, black, and tan, feed on nettles. The species is found in most of the United States and Canada.

Family: Nymphalidae—Wingspan: 1¾–2¼ in (4.5–5.5 cm)
Flight period: Two in most areas from May to October

Cloudless Sulfur
(Phoebis sennae)

Males of this type of butterfly are always bright yellow, and the underside of their wings is lemon-yellow with reddish-brown marks. The wings of the females are paler, ranging from lemon-yellow to cream. Look for this butterfly flying around open spaces like backyards, glades, meadows, and beaches. Its caterpillars are yellow or greenish with black markings and feed on plants, such as partridge pea, senna, and clover. This species is found mainly in the far southeastern United States, but migrates during the summer throughout most of the United States and southeastern Canada.
Family: Pieridae
Wingspan: 2¼–3 in (5.5–7.5 cm)
Flight period: Continuous in the South

Orange Sulfur
(Colias eurytheme)

Also known as the alfalfa butterfly, it's hard to miss this bright orange butterfly. The females are a paler orange than the males, and they have yellow spots on the black border of their wings, while males just have a solid black border. Look for the black spot on the forewings of both males and females. The underside of the hindwing is lemon-yellow. The wings have a pink edge around them. The orange sulfur likes to fly just about anywhere, especially around alfalfa and white clover. It is found in most of the United States and north into Canada.

Family: Pieridae
Wingspan: 1½–2½ in (4–6.5 cm)
Flight period: Many from March to December

Bronze Copper
(Lycaena hyllus)

This butterfly has males and females that are colored differently. Males are dark copper-brown with a purple sheen on their forewings and hindwings that are shiny brown with an orange margin. Females are yellow-orange with dark spots and a brown margin on the forewings, with hindwings that are dark brown with dark spots and an orange margin. Underneath, the forewings of both are mostly orange with a gray edge, and the hindwings are mostly gray with an orange border. Easy to spot because of its size and bright color, the bronze copper can be seen in damp meadows, swamps, and ditches. The caterpillars, which are bright yellowish-green, feed on plants such as dock and knotweeds, which grow in moist areas. This butterfly is found in the central and eastern parts of Canada and the United States.

Family: Lycaenidae
Wingspan: 1¼–1⅞ in (3–4.75 cm)
Flight period: Two to three from May to November

Whirlabout
(Polites vibex)

The males of this butterfly have yellow-orange wings with dark brown markings, while the females have wings that are dull brown with a few light marks on the forewings. The name "whirlabout" comes from this butterfly's habit of flying in rapid circles. Look in grassy habitats for the whirlabout. The caterpillars feed on plants, such as hairy paspalum, and on weedy lawn grasses. The species is found in the southeastern United States, but may stray as far north as Connecticut.
Family: Hesperiidae
Wingspan: 1–1¼ in (2.5–3 cm)
Flight period: Continuous in the South; two in the North from April to September

Spicebush Swallowtail
(Papilio troilus)

This butterfly is mostly brown on the forewings and greenish-blue on the hindwings—creamy-yellow spots frame the wings. There are two bright orange spots on each hindwing, one at the top and one at the bottom. The underside of the wings features two rows of orange-red spots. You will find this butterfly in backyards, woods, meadows, fields, and forests. The dark green caterpillars have four large yellow spots. They eat spicebush, sassafras, and bay. The species is found in the eastern United States.

Family: Papilionidae—Wingspan: 3½–4½ in (9–11.5 cm)
Flight period: From April to October

Tiger Swallowtail
(Papilio glaucus)

This butterfly got its name from its tigerlike black stripes on a yellow background. The hindwings often have a row of blue patches with orange spots. A darker form of the tiger swallowtail exists, in which the females are black with yellow spots. Tiger swallowtails feed in groups from flowers. Their caterpillars start off brown and white, then turn green. Caterpillars of this species feed on broadleaf trees and shrubs, such as willows, birches, and ashes. This butterfly is found in most of North America, except within the Arctic Circle.

**Family:
Papilionidae
Wingspan:
3¼–5½ in
(8–14 cm)
Flight period:
One to three,
from March
to November**

Monarch
(Danaus plexippus)

This butterfly is hard to miss—its great size, bright orange color, and stylish black patterns make it quite noticeable. The monarch has black veins crossing its wings, and a black border sprinkled with white spots. It is one of the most common butterflies and can be seen all over the United States. The caterpillars of the monarch, which are off-white with black-and-yellow stripes, feed on milkweeds—this makes the caterpillar poisonous if eaten. Many a hungry predator has to learn this lesson the hard way! The monarch is found throughout North America south of Alaska and Hudson Bay.

**Family:
Danaidae
Wingspan:
3½–4 in
(9–10 cm)
Flight period:
Several, as it
migrates both
North and South
every year**

A Butterfly Safari

When you go butterfly watching, here are a few items you may want to take in addition to this guide book.

Essential equipment

1 **Magnifying glass:** helps you look at a basking butterfly or a caterpillar on a leaf, close up and in great detail. Or, you could buy a folding magnifying lens and wear it on a cord around your neck.
2 **Glass or plastic jars** with holes bored in the lid: useful if you find a large caterpillar and want to put it somewhere safe while you look at it.
3 **A little paintbrush:** if you want to lift up a caterpillar for a closer look.
4 **Aerial net:** for trapping butterflies and moths temporarily (see opposite page).
5 **Beating tray, sheet, or a pale-colored umbrella:** for investigating trees and bushes (see page 31).

6 **Camera:** to take a quick snapshot of what you see and the habitat in which you found it.
7 **Binoculars:** useful if you want to watch butterflies at a distance or in flight.
8 **Pair of gloves:** some caterpillars can give you a nasty rash from their prickly hairs.
9 **Field notebook and pens or pencils:** always take notes of the weather, the date, where you go, and what you find.
10 **Box of colored pencils:** for field sketches of butterflies.
11 **Lightweight backpack:** this is the most comfortable way to carry your equipment and leaves your hands free.

Field sketches

When you see a butterfly you don't recognize, make a quick sketch in your field notebook. Draw its outline first, then fill in more important details, using your colored pencils. Points to look for are:

- What size was the butterfly? Record a quick estimation of its wingspan.
- Was it one plain color? Write that down.
- Was the butterfly patterned? What colors and shapes were the different patterns?
- Could you see what its antennae were like?
- What kind of flower was it feeding from?
- Did it fly in a particular way?

Also, make a note of the habitat you were in when you spotted the butterfly. This will make it easier for you to look it up in your field guide later.

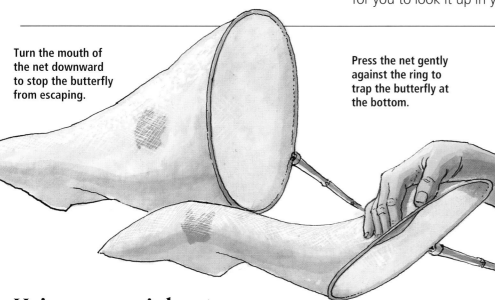

Turn the mouth of the net downward to stop the butterfly from escaping.

Press the net gently against the ring to trap the butterfly at the bottom.

Using an aerial net

It is best to buy a lightweight aerial net from a company that specializes in supplying insect-collecting equipment. The net itself should be made of 28-gauge nylon or muslin. The trick is to turn the mouth of the net sideways once the butterfly is inside. Then the mouth of the net will be covered by material and the butterfly cannot escape.

Hold a butterfly only by its folded wings, very gently, between your thumb and forefinger.

Bogs & Other Wetlands

These damp, watery areas include pond and river banks, marshes, swamps, and peat bogs. The water can be fresh or salt. Bogs have very acidic soil where only certain plants can grow. Many bogs occur in the far north of the United States. You may also find boggy areas in the middle of forests and on mountainsides.

Near wetland areas, you may see large groups of butterflies gathered around mud puddles, drinking the water. This is called mud-puddling, and it provides the butterflies with special minerals. It is a common sight in warmer climates and is an ideal moment to observe them.

Butterflies that live in bog and wetland habitats are particularly at risk from pollution. The places where they live are also at risk from the damage caused when nearby lands are drained for farming or development.

When looking around wetlands for butterflies, tread very carefully—the ground in a wetland can be very soft and squishy. This picture shows butterflies from this section—how many can you recognize?

Beginning clockwise in the upper left-hand corner: hoary elfin, forest copper, clodius parnassian (upper foreground), cinquefoil copper, red-disk alpine, atlantis fritillary, swamp metalmark, forest arctic, purple bog fritillary.

White-spot Alpine
(Erebia disa)

Also known as the spruce bog alpine because it likes moist bogs, this butterfly has wings that are brownish or black, with four eyespots with orange rims on each forewing. The forewing's underside has the same eyespot pattern. A look under the hindwings will show how the butterfly got its name, as there are two white spots here. You may see this butterfly drinking from mud puddles. Its caterpillars feed on meadow grass. The butterfly is found from Alaska to Labrador and Newfoundland, Canada.

♂♀

♀

Family: Nymphalidae
Wingspan: 1¾–2 in (4.5–5 cm)
Flight period: One, from June to July

Forest Arctic
(Oeneis jutta)

Also called the jutta arctic, this dark gray or brown butterfly has a pale orange band running down both sets of wings. Inside the orange markings are black spots. The underside of the hindwing is a blotchy gray and looks a bit like tree bark. This butterfly likes bogland and forests. The caterpillar has olive stripes, and it feeds on cotton grass. This species is found from Alaska to Newfoundland and Labrador in Canada and south to Wyoming in the United States.

♂♀

♂

Family: Nymphalidae
Wingspan: 2–2¼ in (5–5.5 cm)
Flight period: One, from June to August

Red-disk Alpine
(Erebia discoidalis)

Look for the red color on the forewings of this butterfly, which gives it its name. The rest of the wings are blackish-brown with no eyespots. The underside of the wings is a blotched brown and gray. Its caterpillars feed on grasses and sedges in the meadows and prairies in which it lives. It is found from Alaska in the United States to Quebec in Canada and in the northern parts of a few Midwestern states.

Family: Nymphalidae
Wingspan: 1¾–2 in (4.5–5 cm)
Flight period: One, from May to July

♂♀

♂

Western Skipperling

(Oarisma garita)
Also called the garita skipperling, this small butterfly has brownish wings with a gold dusting on them that glints in the light. The edges of the forewings are reddish. The underside of the hindwings is gray with pale orange; forewings are orange at the tip. You will find this butterfly flying around meadows and grasslands, especially where the ground is moist. The caterpillars, green with white lines, feed on various types of grasses. This species is found in southern Canada west of the Great Lakes, and south to Mexico.
Family: Hesperiidae—Wingspan: ¾–1 in (2–2.5 cm)
Flight period: One, from June to August

Aspen Dusky Wing

(Erynnis icelus)

Also called the dreamy dusky wing, this butterfly's wings are rounded and are a gray-brown color. There are gray spots on the forewings, and two rows of pale spots on the hindwings. The underside of the wings looks similar to the top, but the markings are pale. This butterfly can be found in forest clearings and wet meadows. It lays its eggs on a variety of trees. The caterpillars are light green with white speckles and feed on willows, poplars, and birches. The species is found as far north as the Northwest Territories in Canada and south to Georgia and the southwest of the United States.
Family: Hesperiidae
Wingspan: 1–1½ in (2.5–4 cm)
Flight period: One, from April to July

Southern Pearly Eye

(Enodia portlandia)

This butterfly is brownish-tan, with eyespots running down its wings. Note the stacked arrangement of the forewing eyespots. Called the southern pearly eye because it lives mostly in the southeastern United States, you will see this butterfly on tree trunks in woodlands, and also by streams and in backyards. The caterpillars are yellow-green with red-tipped horns, and they feed on cane, a type of grass.
Family: Nymphalidae
Wingspan: 1¾–2¾ in (4.5–7 cm)
Flight period: Three, from April to November

Eyed Brown

(Satyrodes eurydice)

A warm-tan color on top, with rounded wings, the eyed brown has dark spots near the margins of both wings. A look underneath the wings shows a light velvety-brown color with darker, zigzag lines, as well as a row of eyespots with yellow rims. This butterfly likes a damp habitat, such as open meadows, sedge marshes, and wet parts of prairies. The caterpillars, light green with yellow and dark green stripes, feed on sedges. The species is found from the Northwest Territories to Quebec in Canada, and south to the central United States.
Family: Nymphalidae
Wingspan: 1¾–2 in (4.5–5 cm)
Flight period: Two, from June to August

Greenish Blue
(Plebejus saepiolus)

This butterfly's common name comes from the male's wing color, which is silvery-blue with a greenish tinge. Females have two forms, either brown or blue. The underside of the wing for males and females is pale with dark spots. The greenish blue flies in damp, clover meadows in the summer, and also by roadsides, streamsides and in bogs. It is sometimes called the greenish clover blue. The caterpillars, which are greenish or reddish, feed on clover flowers. The species is found from Alaska to Maine and in the northwestern United States.

Family: Lycaenidae
Wingspan: 1–1¼ in (2.5–3 cm)
Flight period: One or two,
from June to July

Hoary Elfin
(Callophrys polios)

This little butterfly has dark brown wings with white and black edging. The underside of the wings features a silvery-gray frosting on the edges, hence the name "hoary," from hoar frost. This butterfly signals the arrival of spring—for it is then that they first appear. They fly in rocky areas, scrub, and heathland. The young green caterpillars feed on bearberry. This species is found in the far northern United States and the Rocky Mountain region, in most of southern and western Canada, and north into Alaska.

Family: Lycaenidae—Wingspan: ¾–1 in (2–2.5 cm)
Flight period: One, from April to June

Two-spot Sedge Skipper
(Euphyes bimacula)

This butterfly has dark brown, pointed wings edged with white. Males have two orange bands on their forewings and females have two small yellowish spots. On the underside of the forewings, both males and females have two yellow spots against a dark orange background. On the underside of the hindwings, you will see a dark tan color with pale veins. Look for this butterfly around bogs, marshes, and sedge meadows. The caterpillars feed on sedges. The species is found in far southeastern Canada, the northeastern United States, and south along the Atlantic Coast.

Family: Hesperiidae
Wingspan: About 1¼ in (3 cm)
Flight period: One, from late June to July

Baltimore
(Euphydryas phaeton)

This butterfly's dark wings have clear orange marks on the outside margins, next to rows of pale yellow spots. The underside looks similar, but has more white and orange markings. The females are larger and more patterned than the males. Named in the 1600's for the first Lord Baltimore, whose coat of arms was of the same colors, this butterfly lives around meadows and bogs. The caterpillars are black with orange stripes and black spines, and they feed on turtlehead, false foxglove, plantain, and white ash. The species is found mainly east of the Mississippi River in the United States.

Family: Nymphalidae
Wingspan: 1¾–2½ in (4.5–6.5 cm)
Flight period: One, from May to August

Pale Tiger Swallowtail
(Papilio eurymedon)

The pale cream background on the wings gives this butterfly its name. Thick black stripes cross the wings, with broad black borders spotted with cream markings. At the bottom of the hindwings are blue and orange markings. The pale tiger flies in patterns around buckthorn bushes. It likes hilltops, where it drinks nectar from mint and thistle plants. The caterpillars, colored green, yellow, and black, feed on mountain plants, including mountain lilac, holly-leaf cherry, and coffeeberry. The species is found from British Columbia in Canada to southern California and New Mexico in the United States.

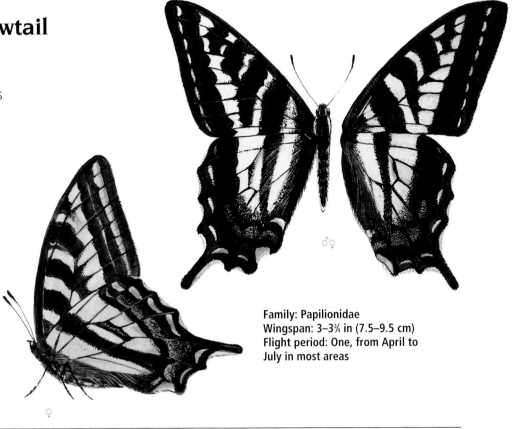

Family: Papilionidae
Wingspan: 3–3¾ in (7.5–9.5 cm)
Flight period: One, from April to July in most areas

Swamp Metalmark
(Calephelis muticum)

This little butterfly has quite pointed brown wings, with fine black spots and dashes. The underside of the wings looks completely different, with a bright orange marking with black patterns. As its name suggests, the swamp metalmark likes wet areas such as swamps. Its pale green caterpillars feed on swamp thistle. This butterfly is found east and south of the Great Lakes to Arkansas in the United States.

Family: Riodinidae
Wingspan: 1–1¼ in (2.5–3 cm)
Flight period: One to two, from June to September

Acadian Hairstreak
(Satyrium acadia)

Also called the northern willow hairstreak, this butterfly is easy to identify, with its dark brown color and one orange spot on each hindwing near the tail. The underside of the wings is silvery-gray, and the male has a blue spot and orange patches near the tail. This butterfly likes to fly around damp fields and meadows, especially where there are willows growing. Their green and yellow caterpillars feed on willows. The species is found across the northern and central United States and in southern Canada.

Family: Lycaenidae
Wingspan: About 1¼ in (3 cm)
Flight period: One, from June to July

Forest Copper
(Lycaena mariposa)

This butterfly's other name is the mariposa copper, from "mariposa," the Spanish word for butterfly. Males of this species look a little different from the females. They have copper-brown wings with a purple tinge and a dark border. Females can be recognized by their bright orange spots, mostly on the forewings. The underside of the hindwings is gray with black patterns, while the forewing underside is copper with a gray margin. You can spot this butterfly in bogs and wet meadows. The species is found from the Yukon in Canada to California and eastward to Wyoming in the United States.
Family: Lycaenidae
Wingspan: 1–1¼ in (2.5–3 cm)
Flight period: One, from July to August

Zigzag Fritillary
(Boloria freija)

Also known as the willow-bog fritillary or Freyja's fritillary—"Freyja" is the Norse goddess of love. This butterfly is dark orange with a black pattern of spots and bands, and it can be easily identified by looking underneath its hindwing. Here, you will see large dashes with white bars near the margin, and a zigzagged red-and-white band in the middle. It flies in forest clearings and willow bogs and also around Arctic tundra. The caterpillars are brown and spiny with creamy spots; they feed on the dwarf and alpine blueberry and black crowberry that grow around its habitat. This species is found from Alaska in the United States to Newfoundland and Labrador, Canada.
Family: Nymphalidae
Wingspan: 1¼–1½ in (3–4 cm)
Flight period: One, from May to July

Cranberry Bog Copper
(Lycaena epixanthe)

Can you guess how this butterfly got its name? It is so called because its caterpillars like to eat cranberries and blueberries, which grow in boglands. Sometimes it is simply called the "bog copper." The male of this little butterfly has brown wings with a purple sheen, while the female is grayish with black specks. The underside of both males and females is much lighter colored, yellow or white, also with black specks. Look near cranberry bushes in bogs, and you will see these butterflies flying around, or perching on the berries. It is found from the Midwest of the United States to Newfoundland and Labrador, Canada.
Family: Lycaenidae
Wingspan: About 1 in (2.5 cm)
Flight period: One, from June to August

Cinquefoil Copper
(Lycaena dorcas)

Also known as the dorcas copper, males of this butterfly are easy to spot, as they have a very bright purple sheen on their wings, which have a wide brown margin. The females have no purple on their wings; instead they have orange and black spots on a dark brown background. Underneath, both males and females are dull yellowish-brown with dark markings. They like to fly around meadows and clearings, as well as bogs, where they visit flowers. The caterpillars feed on cinquefoils, which is how the species got its name. The species is found in Canada in the Northwest Territories eastward to Newfoundland and Labrador, and south to Ohio in the United States.
Family: Lycaenidae
Wingspan: 1–1¼ in (2.5–3 cm)
Flight period: One, from July to August

Broad-winged Skipper

(Poanes viator)

Also called the broad marsh skipper, and true to its name, this butterfly has full, broad wings. The male's wings are dark brown with orange spots on the forewings, and orange with a broad dark margin on the hindwings. Females look similar, except that some have white spots on their forewings. The underside of the hindwings is a rusty-tan color with yellow-orange spots. This butterfly lives around marshland and has gray-brown caterpillars that feed on marsh millet, wild rice, and lake sedge. The species is found in much of the eastern United States.

Family: Hesperiidae
Wingspan: 1¼–1¾ in (3–4.5 cm)
Flight period: One to two, from April to August

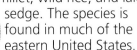

♂♀

Golden Sulfur

(Colias occidentalis)

♀   ♂♀

Also known as the western sulfur, males of this species are lemon-yellow with dark margins, while females are a paler yellow with gray markings on the wings. On the underside of the wings, both males and females are a dark orange-yellow. Look for this butterfly flying by the sea, in meadows and clearings, in pine forests, and on mountain slopes. The caterpillars eat vetch and white sweet clover. This butterfly is found from British Columbia in Canada to California in the United States.

Family: Pieridae
Wingspan: 1½–2 in (4–5 cm)
Flight period: One, from May to August

Clodius Parnassian

(Parnassius clodius)

Also known as the American apollo, this is a butterfly with big rounded wings. In the male, the wings are cream with gray patches. The female has larger gray patches. Both males and females have red spots on the hindwings. The clodius parnassian likes to fly around coastal areas, shaded canyons, and open mountain woods. You may see it flying slowly and deliberately, feeding on nectar from different wild flowers. The caterpillars, usually black with yellow or red spots, feed mainly on the bleeding heart and related plants. The species is found in the west of the United States and Canada.

♂♀

Family: Papilionidae
Wingspan: 2–3 in (5–7.5 cm)
Flight period: One, from June to July

♀

Regal Fritillary
(Speyeria idalia)

A very large butterfly, the regal fritillary has orange forewings with black marks. The females have black hindwings with two rows of cream-colored spots, but the outer row is orange on males. A look at the underside of the hindwings will reveal a deep brown color with lots of pale spots. This butterfly likes to fly around wet meadows and grasslands. Sadly, a lot of the grassland is now being plowed and developed for farmland, so this habitat is disappearing. The caterpillars, yellow, brown, and black with spines, feed on violets. The species is found from the central region to the northeast coast of the United States.

Family: Nymphalidae
Wingspan: 2½–4 in (6.5–10 cm)
Flight period: One, from June to September

Atlantis Fritillary
(Speyeria atlantis)

You can tell the male from the female of this species by the color. Males are deep orange, while females are much paler. Both sexes have black bars, spots, and crescent shapes on their wings, a pattern that continues underneath the forewings. There are silver spots on the underside of the wings. You will find this butterfly around flowered, open spaces, including woodlands, along streams, or in wet meadows. The caterpillars are purplish with stripes and orange spines, and they feed on many types of violets. The species is found in most of Canada and the United States.

Family: Nymphalidae
Wingspan: 1¾–2¾ in (4.5–7 cm)
Flight period: One, from June to August

Viceroy
(Limenitis archippus)

Easy to notice with its rich color and black lattice-pattern of veins, the viceroy also has white-spotted black borders on its wings, and white spots run diagonally across the top of each forewing. This butterfly likes to fly by rivers, marshes, and meadows, as well as roadsides. Its caterpillars are mottled brown or olive in color and like to feed on willows, but they also eat poplars, apples, cherries, and plums. The species is found in most of Canada and the United States.

Family: Nymphalidae—Wingspan: 2½–3 in (6.5–7.5 cm)
Flight period: Two or three, from May to September

Ocellate Fritillary
(Boloria eunomia)

Look for this small butterfly in the bogs and marshes that give it its other name, the bog fritillary. It is orange with dark spots, and the pattern continues under the forewing. On the underside of the hindwing is cream or silver bands with a row of black-rimmed pearly spots. The caterpillars, reddish-brown and spiny, feed on a variety of willows, violets, and other plants that are widely available in boglands. The species is found from Alaska through Canada.

Family: Nymphalidae
Wingspan: 1¼–1½ in (3–4 cm)
Flying period: One,
from June to August

American Painted Lady
(Vanessa virginiensis)

This brightly patterned butterfly has pinkish-orange, black, white, and blue marks on its wings, and a border of white and black. The best way to identify it is to look at the underside of its wings, which is olive-green, black, and white with a pink spot on the forewings and two large blue eyespots on the hindwings. This butterfly is fond of open, heavily flowered sunny spots, such as backyards and streambanks. The caterpillars, black with yellow stripes and white spots, feed on evergreens. The species is found throughout most of the United States and far southern Canada.

Family: Nymphalidae
Wingspan: 1¾–2¼ in (4.5–5.75 cm)
Flight period: Two to four,
from May to October,
continuous in the far South

Purple Bog Fritillary
(Boloria montinus)

This butterfly is dark orange with a very strong black pattern of dots, dashes, and crescents. The underside of the hindwing is a dark color—often purplish—with white marks and a ring of white spots. You can see this butterfly around bogs, tundra, mountainsides, roadsides, and alpine meadows. The caterpillars feed on willows, bistort, and violets. The species is found throughout nearly all of Canada and Alaska and in the Cascade and Rocky mountains of the United States.

Family: Nymphalidae
Wingspan: 1¼-1¾ in
(3–4.5 cm)
Flight period: One,
from June to August

Green Comma
(Polygonia faunus)

Also called the faunus anglewing, this butterfly is a dark orange color with black blotches and yellow spots running alongside a dark margin. It is called the green comma because there are two rows of green bars on a brown background and a silver comma shape on the underside of the wings. This butterfly lives near the banks of streams and in coniferous woodlands and glades. The caterpillars feed on birch, alder, willow, and currant. The species is found from Alaska and most of Canada, south to Carolina and Georgia in the United States.

Family: Nymphalidae
Wingspan: 1¾–2 in
(4.5–5 cm)
Flight period: One,
from May to August

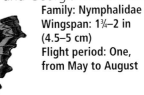

Butterflies To Be

Most insects in the butterfly family spend far more time in the caterpillar and chrysalis stages than in the butterfly stage of life (see pages 4 and 5). Try to find caterpillars or pupae, and you may be able to watch them develop into butterflies.

Beating for caterpillars

One way to find tree- or shrub-dwelling caterpillars is to dislodge them from the branches on which they live. You can do this with a sharp blow from a long stick on the branch. Try striking several different types of trees—some caterpillars will feed only on one type.

1 **Stretch a white sheet out under a low tree branch,** or make a beating tray (see the next page on how to do that). You can also use a pale-colored umbrella turned upside down.
2 **Find a long stick** and hit the base of the branch sharply. Take care not to damage the tree.
3 **Many different insects, including caterpillars, may drop** on to the beating tray.
4 **You might find it easier** if one person holds the beating tray, and the other uses the stick.

Collecting pupae

Looking for pupae (chrysalises) when walking in the country can be a challenging task. Some chrysalises may be buried in the ground or in a pile of leaves, while others may be impossible to spot because they are so well camouflaged (hidden within their surroundings because of their color or pattern).

Just like caterpillars, chrysalises need to be inconspicuous. Some chrysalises look like leaves or twigs. Some even have ragged edges and holes that add to the effect. Tiny silver or gold spots on a chrysalis mimic drops of rain. Other types of chrysalises seem to draw attention to themselves with bright colors. This often indicates they are poisonous and warns off predators.

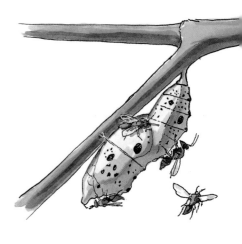

1 **When you have found a chrysalis**, make notes about where you found it. You can also make a colored drawing, noting the way in which it was marked or camouflaged. What was it imitating—a leaf perhaps?

2 **Carefully place the chrysalis in a glass or plastic jar** with holes in the lid (see right).

3 **Take off the lid at home**. Cover the jar with cheesecloth or screening, and put it in the shade.

4 **Check your chrysalis regularly**—every two days or so in the spring.

5 **When it hatches**, take notes on what emerges. You may discover that small wasps crawl out. Many types of insects lay their eggs inside butterfly eggs, on the bodies of caterpillars, or on leaves that the caterpillars then eat. These insects are known as parasites.

Make a beating tray

An easy way to catch caterpillars that live on trees is to make a beating tray. You will need: two bamboo canes about 30 inches (76 centimeters) long, one bamboo cane 36 inches (90 centimeters) long, some white cloth (a piece of old bedsheet will do), strong glue or a stapler, some string or wire, and a long stick.

1 **Place one of the short canes across the top of the long cane** to make a "T" shape and secure it tightly with some string or wire.

2 **Then lay the other short cane across the middle of the long cane** and fix it with wire or string so that it cannot move around.

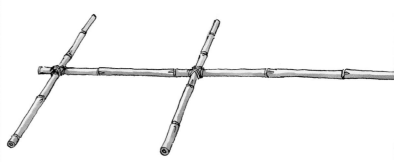

3 **Cut enough white cloth to lay across the bamboo frame** and overlap the edges by 2 inches (5 centimeters) all around.

4 **Lay the cloth on the ground, then lay the frame on top**. Fold the edges of the cloth over the frame and fix it with glue or staples. If this proves difficult, ask an adult to help you. If you use glue, don't use the tray until the glue is dry.

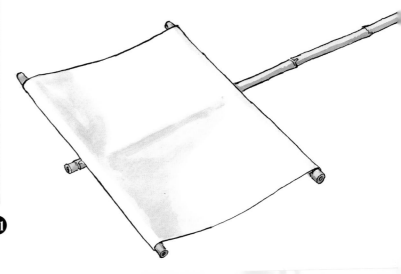

Meadows & Grasslands

Wide, flat, open spaces filled with different types of grasses or flowers are typical of these habitats. These areas are exposed to wind, rain, and sunshine, and provide little shelter for butterflies. Meadows, fields, and pastures are often teeming with wild flowers such as sheep sorrel and clover, to which butterflies such as the small copper are attracted.

Grasslands in the United States are known as prairies, and they occur in a broad belt down the middle of the country. Within this belt, there are three main types of prairie. Towards the East, the prairie is moist and has tall grasses. This region runs from Ohio down to eastern Oklahoma. Towards the West, in the shadow of the Rocky Mountains, the grasslands are dry. In between the two regions, the prairies have medium-height grasses.

Many butterflies that live in prairies lay their eggs on various grasses, so that their caterpillars can eat the grasses once they hatch. Sadly, much of the American prairie is being destroyed both by over-grazing with farm animals and by plowing the land and wild grasses under to grow cultivated grasses. This can mean that a butterfly's favorite plant disappears, leaving it at a loss. This picture shows butterflies from this book—how many can you recognize?

Clockwise from the top left: Melissa arctic, zebra swallowtail, grasshopper satyr, common banded skipper, sara orangetip, swarthy skipper, pink-edged sulfur, greenish blue, least skipperling, prairie skipper, common alpine, purplish copper, European skipperling, and a silver meadow fritillary on the pink flower in the center.

Meadows & Grasslands

Boisduval's Blue
(Plebejus icarioides)

Also known as the common blue, males of this butterfly are silver-blue with dark margins. Females are mostly brown, with some blue at the bases of their wings. On the underside, both males and females are pale gray or cream with black spots. This butterfly is fond of any areas where lupine, a group of plants in the pea family, grows because its caterpillars feed on these plants. Such areas include mountains, valleys, meadows, and roadsides. The species is found from the western United States, north into Canada.

Family: Lycaenidae
Wingspan: 1–1½ in (2.5–4 cm)
Flight period: One, from April to August

♂♀

Orange-margined Blue
(Lycaeides melissa)

♂♀

This butterfly is also known as the Melissa blue. The female has the brown and bluish-gray wings with orange margins that give this butterfly its name. Males look different, with wings of vivid blue with narrow black margins. The underside of the wings is pale with an orange band. Look in alfalfa fields for this butterfly. It is also found in clearings in shrubland and prairie. Their caterpillars eat alfalfa and lupine. The species is found mainly in the central and western areas of the United States and Canada.

Family: Lycaenidae
Wingspan: 1–1¼ in (2.5–3 cm)
Flight period: Two, from May to August

White-M Hairstreak
(Parrhasius m-album)

This is a striking butterfly, with its iridescent bright blue forewings enclosed by a dark margin. Look on the underside of the wings, and you will see the reason for the name: there is a clear "M" shape near the base of each hindwing, in white and black. This area also features orange, black, and blue spots. Each hindwing has two tails, one short and one long. Look for the white-m hairstreak flying rapidly around grassy meadows and clearings in woods, often near oaks. The caterpillars, which are a light yellow-green color, feed on oak trees. The species is found in most of the eastern United States.

♂♀

Family: Lycaenidae
Wingspan: 1¼–1½ in (3–4 cm)
Flight period: Three in the South; two in the North, from February to August

♂

Long-tailed Skipper
(Urbanus proteus)

The long-tailed skipper lives up to its name, with its half-inch-long hindwing tail. The wings are dark brown with a band of white spots across the forewings, and a bright blue-green sheen on the forewing base, hindwings, and body. On the underside the wings are duller, colored pale brown with spots. You will find this beautiful butterfly hard to miss as it flies around watercourses, shores, and backyards. Its caterpillars feed on such plants as legumes and crucifers. The species is found in southern California, Arizona, Texas, Florida, and sometimes along the East Coast as far north as Connecticut.

Family: Hesperiidae
Wingspan: 1½–2 in (4–5 cm)
Flight period: Three or more in Florida, from summer to fall in the North

♂♀

Grizzled Skipper

(Pyrgus centaurea)

This butterfly is also called the alpine checkered skipper, because a checkered margin runs around the edges of its wings, which are black with white spots. The underside of the wings is a brown-olive color with light patches. You will find this butterfly in flowered meadows, glades, and clearings. It lays its eggs on plants in the rose family. The species is found in much of Alaska, Canada, and the mountainous areas of the United States.

♂♀   ♀

Family: Hesperiidae
Wingspan: 1–1¼ in (2.5–3 cm)
Flight period: One, from April to August

♂♀   ♂

Family: Lycaenidae
Wingspan: 1–1¼ in (2.5–3 cm)
Flight period: Continuous in southern California; from May to September elsewhere

Purplish Copper

(Lycaena helloides)

Males of this butterfly have a purplish sheen on their copper-brown wings and a broad, dark edge. The wings of the females are orange, copper, and brown with black marks. The underside of the wings is an orange-yellow color with black spots in both males and females. Look in meadows and alongside streams for this butterfly, from the sea right up to the mountains. The caterpillars, green with yellow stripes, feed on knotweeds, sorrels, and docks. This species is found from Alaska south through western and central Canada and the United States.

Clouded Skipper

(Lerema accius)

This butterfly's pointed wings are dark brown with a row of tiny white spots on the forewings. The underside of the forewings is violet and the hindwings have clouds of light and dark purple. The clouded skipper flies around grassy areas, waysides, and streams. It has white-and-brown caterpillars. The caterpillars' favorite foods include wooly beard-grass, St. Augustine grass, Indian corn, water grass, and paspalum. This species is found in the central, southern, and eastern regions of the United States.

♂♀   ♀

Family: Hesperiidae
Wingspan: 1–1½ in (2.5–4 cm)
Flight period: Several, from February to November in the South

Meadows & Grasslands

Little Wood Satyr
(Megisto cymela)

This brown butterfly has two large black eyespots with yellow rims on each forewing and two more on each hindwing. It may have additional small spots. Darker brown lines cross and border the wings. The little wood satyr likes any grassy, woody area. Its brown caterpillars feed on grasses and sedges. The species is found in the eastern half of the United States and into southeastern Canada.

Family: Nymphalidae
**Wingspan: 1¾–2 in
(4.5–5 cm)**
**Flight period: One,
from May to September**

Zebra Swallowtail
(Eurytides marcellus)

This butterfly is an easy one to spot. It has black-and-white stripes like a zebra. It also features a red stripe on the hindwing, red spots close to the body, and blue spots along the bottom. Other traits that make the zebra swallowtail stand out are its triangular wings, and its very long, pointed hindwing tail. It likes to fly around meadows and near water on riversides and marshes. Its black and yellow striped caterpillars feed on pawpaw. The species is found in most of the eastern United States.

Family: Papilionidae
Wingspan: 2½–3½ in (6.5–9 cm)
**Flight period: Two to four,
from March to December**

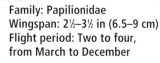

Brown Arctic
(Oeneis chryxus)

This butterfly has light orange-brown wings. Small black eyespots can be seen on the forewings and hindwings. The males have a darker patch across their wings. You may find this butterfly in a variety of places, but it prefers grassy areas. Its caterpillars, which have olive, brighter green, and brown stripes, like to feed on grasses. The species is found in Alaska, most of Canada, the northern Great Lakes region, and through the western mountains of the United States.

Family: Nymphalidae
**Wingspan: 1¾–2 in
(4.5–5 cm)**
**Flight period: One,
from May to August**

Common Alpine
(Erebia epipsodea)

The dark brown wings of this butterfly are rounded, and have orange patches on the forewings and hindwings. Within these patches are black eyespots with white "pupils." You may see the common alpine in several types of habitats, but it prefers grassy areas. Its caterpillars have green stripes and feed on grasses. It is found from Alaska to Manitoba, Canada, and in the western United States south to New Mexico.

Family: Nymphalidae
**Wingspan: 1¾–2 in
(4.5–5 cm)**
**Flight period: One,
from June to August**

Streamside Checkerspot

(Chlosyne nycteis)

♂♀

Also called the silvery checkerspot, this is a mainly dark brown butterfly with orange-and-yellow marks. The underside of the hindwings has yellow, orange, and whitish marks, often with a silvery sheen. This butterfly lives around meadows and woods, as well as by streams. The black-and-orange striped caterpillars have spines and feed on many plants, including sunflowers and black-eyed Susans. The species is found in southern Canada and most of the central and eastern United States.

Family: Nymphalidae—Wingspan: 1½–2 in (3–5 cm)
Flight period: One to four,
from March to September

♂

Buckeye

(Junonia coenia)

You will have no trouble identifying this butterfly. It has four eyespots: two on each forewing, and two on each hindwing. Each eyespot is black, with a yellow rim and bluish center. The background color is brown, and there are orange markings on each wing. Look for the buckeye flying in meadows, and along roadsides and railroad embankments. Its caterpillars are dark colored with orange-and-yellow markings. They feed on lots of different plants, including plantain, figwort, and stonecrop. The species is found throughout the southern United States, and ranges as far north as southeast Canada.

Family: Nymphalidae
Wingspan: 2–2½ in
(5–6.5 cm)
Flight period: Two
to four, continuous in
the South; elsewhere,
from March to October

♂♀

Milbert's Tortoise Shell

(Nymphalis milberti)

♂

This butterfly's alternate name is the fire-rim tortoise shell. The bright orange bands that cross the wings give an appearance of flames. The wings' outside margins are dark; on the hindwing, these margins have a row of blue spots on the inside. The forewings are chocolate brown with red patches going toward the body. The underside of the wings is dull brown and tan. This butterfly flies around waysides, roads, meadows, and streams. The caterpillars, black and spiny with green side stripes, feed on nettles. The species is found from Alaska to Labrador and Newfoundland in Canada, across the central United States, and south to New Mexico.

Family: Nymphalidae
Wingspan: 1¾–2 in (4.5–5 cm)
Flight period: Two or three,
from May to August

♂♀

Common Wood Nymph

(Cercyonis pegala)

This is a large butterfly. Mostly a chocolate-brown color, the wings have large black eyespots, which often lie in a band of orange-yellow. The underside of the hindwing may have up to six eyespots on a mottled-brown background. You may have trouble spotting the common wood nymph as it perches on tree trunks in woodlands—it is well camouflaged against the bark. This nymph also flies along waysides and in grassy areas. Its caterpillars, green with yellow lines, feed on grasses. The species is found in southern Canada and in most of the United States, except for the Southwest.

Family: Nymphalidae
Wingspan: 2–3 in (5–7.5 cm)
Flight period: One,
from June to September

♂♀

Little Glassy Wing
(Pompeius verna)

This is a brown butterfly with glassy white spots on both sides of the forewings. The spots are hard to miss and give the butterfly its name. The underside of the hindwings is darker than above, with yellowish spots. The little glassy wing flies in meadows, pastures, grassy damp places in wooded areas, and roadsides. Its caterpillars, which are tan or green with dark stripes, feed on grasses. This species is found in much of the central and eastern United States.

Family: Hesperiidae—Wingspan: 1–1¼ in (2.5–3 cm)
Flight period: One or more, from April to August

Eastern Cloudy Wing
(Thorybes bathyllus)

Also called the southern cloudy wing, this butterfly's wings are brown, with lighter, checkered edges. The forewings have pale cream marks on them, which are joined together in bars. You can see this butterfly flying through clearings, in dry meadows, and on roadsides. Its caterpillars eat different types of legumes. The species is found in the eastern half of the United States.

Family: Hesperiidae
Wingspan: 1¼–1¾ in (3–4.5 cm)
Flight period: One in the North in June; two in the South, from March to December

Hoary Edge
(Achalarus lyciades)

This butterfly has triangular wings which are blackish-brown in color. There are glassy, yellow-gold marks on the forewings, and checkered margins all around the wings. The name "hoary edge" comes from the big white area on the underside of the hindwing that looks like hoar frost. Look for this butterfly on woodland edges, in backyards, and meadows. Its caterpillars eat several types of legumes. This species is found in much of the eastern and central United States.

Family: Hesperiidae
Wingspan: 1½–1¾ in (4–4.5 cm)
Flight period: One in the North, from May to July; many in the South, from April to December

Long Dash
(Polites mystic)

Both male and female long dashes have wings with orange markings in the middle and a brown border around the outsides. Males have a long black mark almost to the edge of their forewings, which gives the butterfly its name. Female forewings look different because they have yellow marks. The long dash flies in meadows and roadsides, where its caterpillars feed on grasses, including bluegrass. It is found almost coast to coast in southern Canada and the northern United States.

Family: Hesperiidae
Wingspan: 1–1¼ in (2.5–3 cm)
Flight period: One or two, from May to September

Northern Dimorphic Skipper
(Poanes hobomok)

Also called the hobomok skipper, the males and females of this butterfly usually have brown wings with pale yellow-orange patches on the forewings. Males also have a dark marking on their forewings. Sometimes the females look very different and their wings are nearly all dark brown. On the underside of the hindwings of males and females is a yellowish patch. Look for this butterfly flying in grassy areas such as meadows and clearings. Its caterpillars, which are dark green or brown with black spines, feed on grasses. The species is found from the central plains of Canada and the United States to the East Coast.

Family: Hesperiidae
Wingspan: 1–1½ in (2.5–4 cm)
Flight period: One, from May to September

Common Banded Skipper
(Hesperia comma)

Also called the holarctic grass skipper, this little butterfly has brownish wings with tawny-orange patches. Males can be recognized by the black mark on their forewings. The underside of the wings is mottled green and yellow, with a curve of white spots. This butterfly lives in grassy areas, including meadows, foothills, and glades. Its caterpillars feed on various grasses, including pine bluegrass and red fescue. The species is found in Alaska, most of Canada, and the northern and western United States.

Family: Hesperiidae
Wingspan: About 1 in (2.5 cm)
Flight period: One, from June to August

Swarthy Skipper
(Nastra lherminier)

This is a small butterfly with no pattern on its dark brown wings. The forewings are a triangular shape, but the hindwings are rounded. The underside of the wings is chestnut-colored, with yellow veins on the hindwings. The swarthy skipper can be spotted in fields, beaches, and meadows. Its caterpillars feed on prairie beardgrass. The species is found in the eastern, southeastern, and midwestern United States.

Family: Hesperiidae—Wingspan: About 1 in (2.5 cm)
Flight period: Two, in early spring and in fall

Prairie Skipper
(Hesperia ottoe)

Also known as the ottoe skipper, this butterfly's wings are tawny-brown with light brown margins. Males have a clear black mark on their forewings. The underside of the wings is similar to above, but with lighter markings. Look for this butterfly in grassy areas and prairies. The caterpillars feed on various grasses, including fall witchgrass. The species is found in the central United States into southern Canada.

Family: Hesperiidae
Wingspan: 1¼–1¾ in (3–4.5 cm)
Flight period: One, from June to August

Golden-banded Skipper
(Autochton cellus)

It's easy to see the broad, golden bars against a black background that give this butterfly its name. There is also a white spot near the tip of each forewing. Around the edge of each hindwing is a checkered fringe. This big butterfly is found at watersides, and in grassy areas and woodlands. Its caterpillars often feed on hog peanut. The species is found in the eastern, southeastern, and southwestern United States.
Family: Hesperiidae
Wingspan: 1¾–2 in (4.5–5 cm)
Flight period: Two in North, from May to August; more in the South, from February to September

Eastern Sedge Skipper
(Euphyes dion)

Also known as the dion skipper, this butterfly has rounded wings. Males have orange forewings with a brown margin, and the females' forewings are brown with a row of orange spots. Both males and females have brown hindwings with a bright orange "ray" going toward the margin. This agile butterfly flutters around swamps, marshes, and bogs that have sedges and tall grasses. The caterpillars feed on lake sedge and wool grass. The species is found in southeastern Canada and the central and eastern United States.
Family: Hesperiidae
Wingspan: 1¼–1¾ in (3–4.5 cm)
Flight period: One, from July to August in the North, two from May to September in the South

Blazing Star Skipper
(Hesperia leonardus)

Also called the leonardus skipper, the males are not as dark as the females of this butterfly. The males have orange markings on their wings, with a dark brown border. Females are all dark brown except for some pale orange bands on each wing. The underside of the hindwings is chestnut with a row of white spots. This butterfly lives in fields, meadows, prairies, and clearings. Its caterpillars, which are maroon with green marks, feed on bent grass, panic grass, and tumble grass. The species is found in the central and eastern United States and southern Canada.
Family: Hesperiidae—Wingspan: 1–1½ in (2.5–4 cm)
Flight period: One, from August to October

Yellow-patch Skipper
(Polites peckius)

This butterfly is so called because it has yellow patches on its brown and orange wings. The females, which are bigger than the males, are a little darker in color. Underneath, the hindwings have pale yellow bands. Look for this skipper in grassy open spaces like meadows and prairies. Its caterpillars feed on grasses. The species is found from coast to coast, mainly in the northern United States and in Canada.
Family: Hesperiidae
Wingspan: ¾–1 in (2–2.5 cm)
Flight period: One, from May to September

Indian Skipper
(Hesperia sassacus)

♀

This noticeable butterfly has long, triangular wings patterned with orange and brown. The underside of the wings is orange and tan, and the hindwings have a band of pale spots. The Indian skipper flies in fields and meadows, and can be spotted in early springtime. Its caterpillars, which are reddish-brown with light speckles, feed on different types of grasses. The species is found in Canada and east of the Mississippi River in the United States.
Family: Hesperiidae
Wingspan: 1–1½ in (2.5–4 cm)
Flight period: One, from May to July

♂♀

Least Skipperling
(Ancyloxypha numitor)

A small butterfly with rounded wings, the least skipperling is orange and black, with more orange on the hindwings. The underside of the wings is a bright orange-gold with a large dark patch on the forewing. This butterfly is easy to spot flying around grasses in the meadows, pastures, and marshes where it lives. It has light green caterpillars that feed on such plants as marsh millet, bluegrass, and rice. The species is found in most of the region east of the Rocky Mountains in southern Canada and the United States.

Family: Hesperiidae
Wingspan: ¾–1 in (2–2.5 cm)
Flight period: Several, from February to December

♂♀

♀

Arctic Skipperling
(Carterocephalus palaemon)

This butterfly has warm brown wings with rich orange markings. The underside of the hindwings is yellow-orange with several yellow blotches. The arctic skipperling is well known in many countries. It flies around waysides and grassy areas where it sips nectar from wild irises. Its caterpillars are dusky green. The species is found from coast to coast in Canada and across the northern part of the United States.
Family: Hesperiidae
Wingspan: ¾–1¼ in (2–3 cm)
Flight period: One, from May to July

♂♀

Plains Yucca Giant Skipper
(Megathymus streckeri)

The other name for this butterfly, Strecker's giant skipper, comes from the 19th-century butterfly expert Herman Strecker. Large and broad-winged, this butterfly is easy to spot. It has dark brown wings with yellow spots and white marks at the tips of the forewings. The underside of the forewings look similar, but the undersdie of the hindwings is gray-brown with some white spots. This skipper likes to fly around prairies, open woodlands, and yucca plains. Its caterpillars feed on yucca plants. The species is found in the western United States.
Family: Hesperiidae
Wingspan: 2–3 in (5–7.5 cm)
Flight period: One, from May to July

♂

♂♀

Raising Butterflies

A good way to learn more about butterflies is to raise them yourself from caterpillars. Look for caterpillars on leaves, stems, and grasses in the spring and summer. Make sure you collect enough food for your caterpillar.

It's easy to find the right food—just make a note of where you found the caterpillar and what plant it was on, so you can return and collect more food when you need it. (Take a stalk of the plant with some leaves if you are not sure you will recognize it again when you return.)

Cages

To make a cage, use:

- a shoebox covered with window screening on top, or
- a sheet of clear plastic rolled into a tube standing in a plastic tub with soil in the bottom, or
- a large clear jar (2 pints [1 liter] or more)

For the last two, cover the top with cheesecloth and secure it with a rubber band.

How to raise caterpillars

1 **When you find a caterpillar, break off the piece of the plant** you found it on and gently place it in your prepared container. When the caterpillar is newly hatched and tiny, it won't need a big cage. A jar or plastic box lined with newspaper will do.

2 **Remember that your caterpillar will need new leaves EVERY day.**

3 **When it grows bigger** (after the first molt), you will need to transfer the caterpillar to a more suitable container (see below). **Be careful!** Move your caterpillar using the tip of a small paintbrush. This will help you to avoid damaging it, and it also prevents the caterpillar from damaging you **(some caterpillars have stinging hairs).** Place the caterpillar on the food plant in the new cage.

4 **Now you can pick bigger pieces of the food plant and place them in a jar of water to keep them fresh.** Put a twig or stick in for perching, and for the caterpillar to hang its chrysalis from, then put the jar in the cage. Make sure you cover the top of the jar to prevent the growing caterpillar from falling into the water. Keep putting fresh plants in every other day.

5 **A caterpillar may take a while to enter its chrysalis**—and sometimes it has to spend the winter in the chrysalis.

8 **When the adult butterfly has struggled out of the chrysalis,** remove the top of the cage and put it outside. The butterfly will fly away when its wings have dried and expanded.

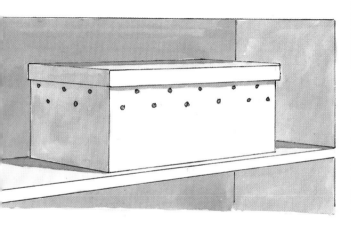

6 **Remember to label the cage** with the date, species name, etc.

7 **If the caterpillar pupates in soil or sand, spray the soil occasionally with water** as it must be damp—otherwise the pupa might die.

What to watch for

When you are raising a caterpillar, make note of the following things. Also, try sketching the different stages in the butterfly's life as they occur.

- What food plant did you find your caterpillar on?
- How many times did the caterpillar molt?
- Did any of the caterpillars make a leaf tent?
- How long did the caterpillar take to enter its chrysalis?
- What did the chrysalis look like? Could you see the butterfly's wings through the skin of the chrysalis, and at what stage?
- How long did it take for the butterfly to break out of the chrysalis?
- How long did it take the butterfly to dry and expand its wings?
- Can you identify the butterfly?

Meadows & Grasslands

Grasshopper Satyr
(Neominois ridingsii)

This butterfly is also known as Riding's satyr. The name grasshopper satyr comes from its patterns, which are like those on a grasshopper. You will have no problem identifying this butterfly, as no other butterfly in North America has such a color or pattern. Different shades of gray cover its wings, while cream-colored bands cross the wings from top to bottom. There are several black eyespots with white pupils on each forewing. The underside of the wings is a speckled gray. Its caterpillars are reddish with green bands and feed on grasses. The species is found from central Canada to the southwestern United States.

Family: Nymphalidae
Wingspan: 1½–2 in (4–5 cm)
**Flight period: One,
from June to August**

Gray Copper
(Lycaena xanthoides)

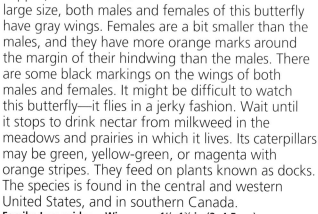

Also called the great gray copper, because of its large size, both males and females of this butterfly have gray wings. Females are a bit smaller than the males, and they have more orange marks around the margin of their hindwing than the males. There are some black markings on the wings of both males and females. It might be difficult to watch this butterfly—it flies in a jerky fashion. Wait until it stops to drink nectar from milkweed in the meadows and prairies in which it lives. Its caterpillars may be green, yellow-green, or magenta with orange stripes. They feed on plants known as docks. The species is found in the central and western United States, and in southern Canada.

Family: Lycaenidae—Wingspan: 1¼–1¾ in (3–4.5 cm)
Flight period: One, from May to August

Northern Cloudy Wing
(Thorybes pylades)

Rounded, brown wings with white marks on the forewings are the features of this butterfly. Checkered fringes run around the edges of the wings. The northern cloudy wing is very common, and flies in open woods, roadsides, meadows, fields, and clearings. Its caterpillars feed on legumes, where they make silken nests. The species is found in much of central Canada and the United States.

Family: Hesperiidae
Wingspan: 1¼–1¾ in (3–4.5 cm)
**Flight period: Two,
from March to
December**

Arctic Blue
(Agriades glandon)

Male arctic blues are blue-gray or sometimes greenish; females are orange-brown. The underside of the wings is brown with bright white markings and black spots. This butterfly, also called the high mountain blue, flies in tundra and mountain meadows, prairies, and open woodland. Its caterpillars probably feed on rock jasmine and shooting star in the farther south, and diapensia in the Arctic. They may also eat blueberry. The species is found in Alaska, nearly all of Canada, and the mountainous areas of the western United States.

Family: Lycaenidae
Wingspan: ¾–1 in (2–2.5 cm)
**Flight period: One,
from June to August**

Wolf-face Sulfur

(Eurema mexicana)

This butterfly has a marking like a long-snouted wolf's face on its dark forewing tip. The male has white wings with a yellow mark at the top of the hindwings, and the female has pale yellow wings. You may see this butterfly, also called the Mexican yellow, around meadows, desert chaparral, and mountain canyons. Its caterpillars feed on senna plants. The species is found in Mexico, in the southwestern United States, and as far north as Manitoba, Canada.

Family: Pieridae
Wingspan: 1½–2 in (4–5 cm)
Flight period:
From March to
November

♂♀

Sara Orangetip

(Anthocaris sara)

Also called the western orangetip, it is easy to see how this butterfly got its name. It has a bright orange tip surrounded by a black margin on each of its forewings. Its coloring may be confusing, as males can be either white or yellow, but females are always yellow. A look at the underside of the hindwings will reveal a mottled grass-green color. The orangetip flies around meadows, mountain roads, by streams, and even in desert canyons. Its caterpillars are moss-green and like to feed on many kinds of mustard plant. The species is found in the west of Canada and the United States.

Family: Pieridae
Wingspan: 1¼–1½ in (3–4 cm)
Flight period:
From February to July

♂♀

♂

Coral Hairstreak

(Satyrium titus)

Males and females of this butterfly look different from one another. The male has very dark brown pointed wings, with light reddish spots on the hindwing margin. Females have rounded wings, which are lighter brown, and they feature red spots along the hindwing margin. The underside of both males and females is lighter brown with black spots rimmed with white, and bright orange spots all along the hindwing margin. The coral hairstreak flies rapidly through meadows, lighting on flowers to sip nectar in shrubby and wooded areas. Its yellow-green caterpillars often feed on unripe plums and wild cherries. The species is found in most of the United States and Canada.

♀

Family: Lycaenidae
Wingspan: 1–1¼ in (2.5–3 cm)
Flight period: One,
from June to August

♂♀

Rosy Marble

(Euchloe olympia)

This chalky white butterfly, which is also called the Olympia marblewing, has gray marks on its wings and a rosy color both above and below the base of its hindwings. There is also a mottled green underneath the hindwing, which is good camouflage when this insect folds its wings against greenery. You may see this butterfly fluttering around open woods and meadows, as well as foothills and dunes. Its caterpillars are bright green, striped with gray and yellow, and feed on buds and flowers of mustard plants. The species is found mainly in the central and eastern United States.

Family: Pieridae
Wingspan: 1½–1¾ in (4–4.5 cm)
Flight period: One, from March to June

♀

♂♀

Ringlet
(Coenonympha tullia)

An orange-brown color on top, this butterfly has eyespots on both sides of its wings. The eyespots on the underside are black-and-yellow rimmed, with white dots in the middle. You can spot the ringlet in grassy areas. Its caterpillars feed on grasses or rushes. The species is found in Alaska, through most of Canada, and in the northern and western United States.
Family: Nymphalidae
Wingspan: 1–2 in (2.5–5 cm)
Flight period: One or two, from March to October

Black-vein Skipper
(Anatrytone logan)

Males and females of this butterfly have bright orange wings with dark borders and veins, but females are larger and darker, with darker veins and a wide border. The underside of the wings is yellow-gold with black edges. You can spot this skipper on the edge of woodlands and in grassy areas. The caterpillars are black and white. Also known as the Delaware skipper, this butterfly is found in most of the central and eastern United States and in southern Canada.

Family: Hesperiidae
Wingspan: 1–1½ in (2.5–4 cm)
Flight period: One, from July to August in the North, many from February to October in the far South

Sachem
(Atalopedes compestris)

Both males and females of this butterfly have tawny-orange and brown wings. It is easy to tell which ones are the males, as they have a huge black mark on their wings. Females can be recognized by the two bright spots on their forewings. On the underside, the forewings are tawny, and the hindwings are dusky yellow. Look for the sachem flying in pastures and fields, as well as in backyards. Lots of sachems appear in the summertime. Its caterpillars feed on different types of grasses. The species is found in much of the United States.
Family: Hesperiidae
Wingspan: 1–1½ in (2.5–4 cm)
Flight period: Three in the South, covering most of the year

European Skipperling
(Thymelicus lineola)

This butterfly has dark orange wings with black veins toward the edges and a dark border. The underside of the forewings is orange and of the hindwings is copper or greenish in color. The European skipperling was brought from Europe to America in 1910. It flies around meadows and pastures, and its green caterpillars feed on timothy hay. It is found mainly in the eastern part of Canada and the United States.
Family: Hesperiidae
Wingspan: ¾–1 in (2–2.5 cm)
Flight period: One, from June to August

Hairy Dusky Wing
(Erynnis persius)

Also known as the persius dusky wing, this brownish-black butterfly has small glassy dots on its forewing tips. It is called "hairy" because males have long gray hairs on their forewings. The hindwings of males and females have rows of black markings. The underside of the wings is lighter brown. A fairly rare butterfly, the hairy dusky wing flies in grasslands and open woodlands. Its caterpillars, which are light green and hairy, feed on lupine in the East and golden banner in the West. The species is found mostly in western Canada.

Family: Hesperiidae
Wingspan: 1–1½ in (2.5–4 cm)
Flight period: One or two,
from April to September

Melissa Arctic
(Oeneis melissa)

Also called the mottled arctic, this gray-brown butterfly has few markings on top, but the underside of the hindwing features a dark gray mottled pattern. Its wings are almost transparent, so it is well camouflaged against lichen-covered rocks in the arctic meadows where it lives. The caterpillars of this butterfly are green with blue and yellow stripes. They feed on grasses and sedges. The species is found in mountainous areas of the western United States.

Family: Nymphalidae—Wingspan: 1¾–2 in (4.5–5 cm)
Flight period: One, from June to August

Brown-rim Skipper
(Atrytone arogos)

Another name for this butterfly is the beard-grass skipper. Males have tawny-orange wings with dark brown margins; females have broader margins on their wings and not as much orange color. The underside of the wings is lighter, sometimes even bright yellow. The brown-rim skipper lives and lays its eggs in beard-grass fields. Once hatched, the caterpillars feed on the grasses. The species is found in the central and southeastern parts of the United States.

Family: Hesperiidae
Wingspan: 1–1¼ in (2.5–3 cm)
Flight period: One in the
North, from June to July,
two in the South from
March to May and from
August to September

Polixenes Arctic
(Oeneis polixenes)

This butterfly is also called the banded arctic because the undersides of its hindwing are marked with a broad dark band. Apart from this, the wings are a plain grayish-brown and almost transparent. This butterfly is hard to spot in the grassy areas where it lives. Its caterpillars feed on arctic and alpine grasses. The species is found in far northern Canada, in Alaska, and in a few mountainous areas in the United States.

Family: Nymphalidae
Wingspan: 1½–1¾ in
(4–4.5 cm)
Flight period: One,
from June to August

Variegated Fritillary
(Euptoieta claudia)

Orange-brown colors with black patterns of spots and stripes is the hallmark of this butterfly. The pattern continues on the underside of the wings, but it is fainter. Females of this butterfly are bigger than the males. The variegated fritillary likes to fly around open grassy areas such as fields, grasslands, and meadows. Its caterpillars, colored white with red bands and black spines, will eat almost anything, from violets and pansies to plantain and passion flowers. The species is found from Canada to the southern United States.

Family: Nymphalidae
Wingspan: 1¾–2¼ in (4.5–5.75 cm)
Flight period: Continuous in the South; one, from March to December, in the North

Great Plains Checkerspot
(Chlosyne gorgone)

Also called the gorgone checkerspot, this butterfly is orange, yellow, and brown, with a row of black spots on the hindwing. The underside of the hindwing is gray with heavy black marks. It flutters around flowery meadows, waysides, and woodlands. The caterpillars are orange-red with black bands and feed on several plants, including sunflowers. The species is found in the central parts of Canada and the United States.

Family: Nymphalidae
Wingspan: 1¼–1¾ in (3–4.5 cm)
Flight period: One, from May to September

Meadow Fritillary
(Boloria bellona)

This butterfly has dark orange-brown wings with black dashes and dots. The underside of the hindwing is orange-brown, gray, and lilac. The meadow fritillary can be spotted in damp meadows or near any marshy spot. The caterpillars, purplish-black with black and yellow marks and brown spines, feed on violets. It is found from the Yukon to Quebec in Canada to the southeastern United States.

Family: Nymphalidae
Wingspan: 1¼–2 in (3–5 cm)
Flight period: Three, from May to September

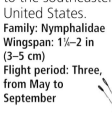

American Copper
(Lycaena phlaeas)

This butterfly has three different names: the American copper because of where it lives, the small copper because of its small size, and the flame copper because of its bright fiery color. The forewings are a bright copper color on top with dark spots and a dark margin. The hindwings are brown with copper borders. The caterpillars, which are green- and rose-colored, feed on sheep sorrel, curly dock, or mountain sorrel. The species is widely distributed in North America, even within the Arctic Circle.

Family: Lycaenidae
Wingspan: 1–1¼ in (2.5–3 cm)
Flight period: One or several, from April to October in the South.

Pearl Crescentspot
(Phyciodes tharos)

This butterfly is an orange color with dark margins around its wings and dark markings. Look for the white crescent-shaped marks along the hindwing borders. The crescentspot likes to fly over meadows, fields, and prairies, quite near the ground. The caterpillars are spiny and brown with yellow bands. They feed on the leaves of asters. The species is found in much of the United States and part of southern Canada.

Family: Nymphalidae
Wingspan: 1–1½ in (2.5–4 cm)
Flight period: Several,
from April to November

Silver Meadow Fritillary
(Boloria selene)

This is a small butterfly with black-marked orange wings. It is also called the silver-bordered fritillary because the underside of its hindwing has rows of metallic silver spots. True to its name, this butterfly likes meadows, but it can also be seen around bogs, near woodlands, or among plains. Its caterpillars are brownish-black with yellow spines and feed on violets. The species is found in Alaska, much of Canada, and as far south as Arizona.

Family: Nymphalidae
Wingspan: 1½–2 in (4–5 cm)
Flight period: One to three,
from May to October

Field Crescentspot
(Phyciodes campestris)

This blackish-brown butterfly is speckled with orange and yellow patches and spots. Underneath, the forewing is pale orange, the hindwing is pale tan, and both have dark patches. This is the crescentspot you are most likely to see, as it is the most common one in North America. Look for it flying about meadows, forest clearings, and swamps and fields. Its spiny caterpillars feed on aster leaves. The species is found from Alaska through Canada and into New Mexico in the United States.

Family: Nymphalidae—Wingspan: 1¼–1½ in (3–4 cm)
Flight period: Four, from April to October

Great Spangled Fritillary
(Speyeria cybele)

This butterfly is so called because of the silver "spangles" on the underside of the hindwing. The great spangled fritillary is orange-brown, with dark patterns of dots, dashes, and crescents. Look for it flying swiftly, pausing to drink nectar from flowers. It flies around meadows and woodland glades. The caterpillars, which are tiny with black spines, feed on violets. The species is found from the East to the West coasts of the United States, and in southern Canada.

Family:
Nymphalidae
Wingspan:
2¼–3 in
(5.75–7.5 cm)
Flight period:
One, from
June to September

Pink-edged Sulfur
(Colias interior)

Yellow wings with bright pink fringes identify this butterfly. You can distinguish the male by the thick black borders on its wings; females have little or no border. Both males and females have an orange spot on each hindwing. Look around flowery meadows, woodlands, and also marshes and bogs for this butterfly. Its caterpillars are bright yellow-green with lighter back stripes and red-edged side stripes. They feed on blueberries. The species is found in most of the northern United States and in southern Canada.

Family: Pieridae
Wingspan: 1½–1¾ in (4–4.5 cm)
Flight period: One, from June to August

Common Sulfur
(Colias philodice)

Males of this type of butterfly are always yellow with a thick black border, but females are sometimes white with a yellow-spotted black border. Both males and females have an orange spot in the middle of each hindwing. The underside is a greenish-yellow. Look for the common sulfur in flowery meadows, pastures, forests, and deserts. Its caterpillars are bright green and feed on plants in the pea family, especially clovers. The species is found in most of the United States and Canada.

Family: Pieridae
Wingspan: 1½–1¾ in (4–4.5 cm)
Flight period: Several from March to December

Family: Pieridae
Wingspan: 1–1½ in (2.5–4 cm)
Flight period: Continuous in the South, from May to October in the North.

Little Sulfur
(Eurema lisa)

This butterfly is also called the little yellow because of its color. Its wings have black borders, which are more strongly patterned in the males. Females are often paler yellow than males. The little sulfur flies around open areas like roadsides and fields. Its caterpillars are green with white stripes and feed on senna, partridge pea, clovers, and hog peanut. The species is found in the eastern, central, and southwestern United States.

Black-dust Skipper

(Hesperia viridis)

This butterfly is orange with wide brown borders on its wings. Females are brighter in color than males. The underside of the forewings is similar, but that of the hindwings is bright olive-green, which is why this butterfly is also called the green skipper. It lives in prairies and canyons. The caterpillars feed on grass. The species is found in the western and southwestern United States.

Family: Hesperiidae
Wingspan: 1–1½ in (2.5–4 cm)
Flight period: Two, from April to October

Fiery Skipper

(Hylephila phyleus)

This butterfly gets its name from its bright yellow-orange color. Males have patterned wings with a zigzagged border, and females have long wings and large orange spots. The fiery skipper lives in grassy areas such as clearings, waysides, and forest edges. Its caterpillars feed on grasses. The species is found throughtout the eastern and southwestern United States.

Family: Hesperiidae
Wingspan: 1–1¼ in (2.5–3 cm)
Flight period: Two or more, from April to December

Southern Dimorphic Skipper

(Poanes zabulon)

Males of this butterfly are yellow-orange above and below with brown spots. Females are blackish with glassy spots and a violet tinge on the underside. This butterfly flies around grassy areas such as meadows and scrubland. The caterpillars feed on grasses, including tumble grass. The species is found mostly east of the Mississippi River in the United States.

Family: Hesperiidae
Wingspan: 1–1½ in (2.5–4 cm)
Flight period: Two, from May to August

Ultraviolet Sulfur

(Colias alexandra)

This butterfly is also known as Queen Alexandra's sulfur, after a queen of England. The male of this type of butterfly is bright lemon-yellow with a thick black border on its wings. The female can be yellow or white, and her markings are lighter than the male's. Both males and females have a black spot on each forewing. The underside of the hindwings is green with a silvery spot. This butterfly can be seen around clearings, meadows, and roadsides. The caterpillars, colored green with lengthwise stripes, feed on vegetable plants, including wild pea. The species is found in the Rocky Mountains and the Great Plains of the United States and Canada.

Family: Pieridae
Wingspan: 1½–2½ in (4–6.5 cm)
Flight period: One, from June to July

Butterfly Garden

If you have a yard, you can do a lot to make it attractive to butterflies. This will not only help the butterflies, it will also make your yard a very colorful place. The best way to start is by planting flowers that make a lot of nectar. Many butterflies love to sip nectar with their long tongues, which are a bit like straws. Trees, too, can attract butterflies—some butterflies like to drink tree sap or eat rotten fruit on the ground.

Don't forget about the caterpillars—if you grow their food plants, it will encourage female butterflies to lay their eggs there. Another important thing to remember—don't use pesticides in your garden! These can be poisonous to butterflies.

Butterfly watching

Watching how butterflies and caterpillars behave in the field can be interesting and exciting. You can get a really good look at them if they are busy feeding or drinking, so a flowery garden is one of the best places to start. Approach the butterfly quietly and be careful not to make any sudden movements that would frighten it away.

Caterpillars can't fly away, but they can look like something else—such as leaves, twigs, or even bird droppings. You'll need to look carefully to find caterpillars. **Beware of touching hairy caterpillars—some can give you a nasty rash.**

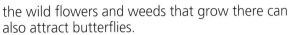

Flowers and trees

Adult butterflies will feed on many different flowers. Most prefer flowers of such colors as pink, mauve, and purple. Large butterflies prefer to feed from tall flowers, while smaller types like low-growing flowers. Butterflies also like flowers with flat tops or large petals that are easy to land on. If you let a piece of garden go wild, the wild flowers and weeds that grow there can also attract butterflies.

Nettles: Red admirals lay their eggs on nettles, as this is their caterpillars' food plant.

Daisies: Don't get rid of your daisies—butterflies such as the western skipper sip the nectar from daisies.

Clover: This is a food plant for many types of caterpillars.

Other good flowering plants to attract butterflies are sunflowers lilacs, passion flowers, pansies, marigolds, and rock roses.

Buddleia: The flowers this shrub produces are so popular with butterflies that it is often called the butterfly bush. The pipevine swallowtail is an example of a buddleia-loving butterfly.

The leaves of trees are food plants for many types of caterpillars. Favorite trees include: oak, birch, willow, sycamore, walnut, cherry, and poplar.

When is a butterfly not a butterfly?

When it's a moth, of course! There are even more moths than butterflies around—more than 87,000 species worldwide—but as a general rule, they are not as noticeable as butterflies. Here are some ways to tell them apart, but remember there are exceptions to all these tests:

- Butterflies fly during the day—moths fly at night
- Butterflies are brightly colored—moths are usually drab
- Butterflies rest with their wings held vertically—moths rest with them held flat
- The antennae of most butterflies end in small clubs (see page 6)

Deserts & Mountains

Hot, dry, sandy deserts do not seem like suitable places for butterflies, but many butterflies live there all the same. Don't expect to see butterflies during the hottest time of the day, however, as they usually shelter from the heat of the midday sun. They venture out when it is cooler, in the early morning or late in the evening.

The largest desert regions in the United States are the Great Basin—which extends across parts of California, Idaho, Nevada, Oregon, Utah, and Wyoming—and the Mojave Desert in southern California. The best places to look for butterflies are near plants or around water holes.

High up in the clouds, often wind-swept and cold, mountains also seem an unlikely home for butterflies. And it is true that the butterflies that live there have to be hardy. The weather often changes quickly from sunny and tranquil to windy and snowy. When the sun is out, mountain butterflies make the most of it: they sunbathe with their wings outstretched. They often have dark-colored wings to absorb the heat quickly. Hairy bodies also help to keep in the precious warmth should the weather change suddenly. Notice the way that the butterflies of these areas fly—close to the ground and in short bursts. This is to combat the fierce winds that often sweep over mountain tops. This picture shows butterflies from this section—how many can you recognize?

Clockwise from the upper left corner: checkered white, cliff swallowtail, yucca giant skipper, sylvan hairstreak, orange hairstreak, dainty sulfur, and a pale crescent in the center below the cliff swallowtail.

Sylvan Hairstreak
(Satyrium sylvinus)

Males of this species, which is also known as the western willow hairstreak, have light gray to brown wings, while the females are darker. Both males and females have some reddish color near the base of their hindwings. They usually have tails, but some of these butterflies are tailless. The underside of the wings is gray to white-gray with black markings. This butterfly can often be seen near willow trees, which are their caterpillars' favorite food plant. The species is found on the Pacific Coast of Canada and the United States and east to New Mexico.

Family: Lycaenidae
Wingspan: 1–1¼ in (2.5–3 cm)
Flight period: One,
from May to August

Mesquite Metalmark
(Apodemia palmerii)

This butterfly is named for the honey mesquite plant that its caterpillars eat in the desert. Also called Palmer's metalmark or the gray metalmark, this butterfly is small with a gray-brown background on its wings. The wings are covered with white and orange spots and dashes, which give a bright pattern. The species is found from southern California to west Texas in the United States.

Family: Riodinidae
Wingspan: ¾–1 in (2–2.5 cm)
Flight period: Three,
from April to November

Redhead Sooty Wing
(Staphylus ceos)

Also called the goldenheaded sooty wing because of its orange head, this butterfly is otherwise dull in color. Both the top and underside of its wings, which are very rounded, are dark brown. It flies in canyons, at the bottom of valleys, and in foothills. The species is found in the southwestern United States.

Family: Hesperiidae
Wingspan: 1–1¼ in (2.5–3 cm)
Flight period: Several,
from March to November

Columbine Dusky Wing
(Erynnis lucilius)

A small butterfly, the columbine dusky wing gets its name from the wild columbine plant that its caterpillar eats. The butterfly has short, rounded wings, which are dark with little spots on the forewings and bands of darker marks. The hindwings are dark brown with some tan spots. You will see this butterfly on the edges of woodlands, in glades, and in upland areas. The species is found in the central and eastern regions of Canada and the United States.

Family: Hesperiidae
Wingspan: 1–1¼ in (2.5–3 cm)
Flight period: Two or three,
from May to August

White-veined Skipper
(Hesperia uncas)

Also called the uncas skipper, this butterfly is tawny-brown with whitish marks on the forewing. You can spot the males by the black mark they have on the forewings. The underside of the forewing is paler than the top of the wing. The hindwing underside has several silvery-white marks and white veins, hence the butterfly's name. Its caterpillars feed in the grassland areas where this butterfly lives. It is found in the central and western United States and in south-central Canada.

♂♀

Family: Hesperiidae
Wingspan: 1–1¾ in (2.5–4.5 cm)
Flight period: Two or more, from May to September

Yucca Giant Skipper
(Megathymus yuccae)

A large butterfly, the yucca giant skipper has black wings with yellow marks and borders. A good identification mark to look for is the white spot at the top of the forewings. Another feature is the big, plump body, which is black or dark brown. Look for this butterfly in deserts, scrubby woodlands, and old fields. As the name suggests, its caterpillars feed on yucca plants. They make silk shelters in the plants by strapping leaves together. The species is found in the southern United States.

Family: Hesperiidae
Wingspan: 2–3 in (5–7.5 cm)
Flight period: One, from January to June

♂♀

Cliff Swallowtail
(Papilio indra)

This butterfly is also known as the short-tailed black swallowtail because it has shorter "tails" than do most swallowtails. Its wings are mainly black, with pale yellow spots and bands. There are faint blue markings on the hindwings, along with orange eyespots. You may spot this butterfly around mountains, canyons, and cliffs, where males often take part in exciting flight displays, battering each other in the air to win territory or a mate. The caterpillars feed on carrot or parsley plants. The species is found on the west coast of the United States, east to Nebraska.

♂♀

Family: Papilionidae
Wingspan: 2¼–3½ in (5.75–9 cm)
Flight period: One to two, from March to August

Western Tiger Swallowtail
(Pterourus rutulus)

Both the top and underside of the wings of this butterfly are lemon-yellow, with black tigerlike stripes across its wings, and thick black margins with yellow spots. You can also see orange and blue markings at the base of its hindwings. You will probably spot this butterfly in the Western States, as it rarely flies east of the Rocky Mountains. The green caterpillars feed on trees, such as willow, poplar, and sycamore. The species is found in southern British Columbia, Canada, and in the western United States.

Family: Papilionidae
Wingspan: 2¾–4 in (7–10 cm)
Flight period: From February to November

Orange Hairstreak
(Satyrium behrii)

Named for its orange wings, this butterfly is also called Behr's hairstreak. The wings have dark margins at the edges. The underside of the wings is gray with rows of black and white speckles. This butterfly likes dry areas. The caterpillar, green with white, yellow, or dark green stripes, feeds on antelope brush. You are most likely to see the butterflies near this plant. The orange hairstreak is found in British Columbia, Canada, and in the western United States.

Family: Lycaenidae
Wingspan: 1–1¼ in (2.5–3 cm)
**Flight period: One,
from June to July**

Dainty Sulfur
(Nathalis iole)

The tiny size of this butterfly has earned it the name dainty sulfur, as well as its other name, dwarf yellow. Both males and females have yellow wings with dark forewing tips, which are more strongly patterned on the female. The female may also have an orange color on the hindwings. The underside of the wings is greenish-yellow to gray, with black spots. Look for the dainty sulfur in waysides and canyons, or flying along rivers or railroad tracks. Its caterpillars, of a deep green color with purple back stripes and black and yellow side stripes, feed on weeds, marigolds, and daisies. The species lives in the southern half of the United States. It migrates, however, through most of the United States and into Manitoba, Canada.

Family: Pieridae
**Wingspan: ¾–1 in
(2–2.5 cm)**
**Flight period:
Any month in the South;
later farther North**

♂♀

♀

Crossline Skipper
(Polites origenes)

You can tell the male crossline skippers from the females by the males' brighter forewings. Both males and females have orange-brown wings. The underside of the wings is dull brown, with spots on the hindwing. You can see this butterfly in canyons as well as in dry meadows, open woodland, and prairies. Its caterpillars are dark brown with whitish markings. They feed on desert bunchgrass. The species is found in most of the eastern and central United States.

Family: Hesperiidae
Wingspan: 1–1¼ in (2.5–3 cm)
Flight period: One, from June to August

Yellow-dust Skipper
(Hesperia pahaska)

This butterfly is orange with a brown border round its wings. The yellow dusting on the forewings gives it its name. The underside of the forewing looks similar to above, but the hindwing underside is brownish with silver-white spots. This butterfly, also known as the pahaska skipper, is fond of grassy areas and canyons, and its caterpillars feed on grasses. It is found in the Rocky Mountain regions of southern Canada and the United States and in the deserts of the southwestern United States.

♂♀

Family: Hesperiidae
Wingspan: 1¼–1½ in (3–4 cm)
Flight period: Two, from May to September

Black-veined Skipperling
(Adopaeoides prittwitzi)

Above, the wings of this butterfly are bright orange, with black veins. The underside of the wings is light yellow to reddish-gold. There is a yellow "ray" on the hindwing that gives this butterfly its other name, the sunrise skipperling. This species can be spotted in dry areas such as deserts and scrubland, near sources of water, such as springs. It is found in the southwestern United States.

Family: Hesperiidae
Wingspan: 1–1¼ in (2.5–3 cm)
Flight period: Two, from May to June, and in September

♂♀

Arrowhead Skipper
(Stinga morrisoni)

This butterfly is also called Morrison's silver spike from its discoverer, H. K. Morrison. Its forewings are a tawny-orange with dark borders. The hindwings are brown. On the underside, the forewings are similar, but the hindwings are rust-brown, crossed by silvery marks that look like an arrowhead. This butterfly lives in mountain valleys and moist meadows, pine forests, foothills, and hilltops. It is found in the southwestern United States.

♂♀

Family: Hesperiidae
Wingspan: 1–1¼ in (2.5–3 cm)
Flight period: One, from May to mid-June in the Rockies, but later farther south

♀

Spring White
(Pontia sisymbrii)

This butterfly is one of the first to appear in the spring. Its wings are mostly white with brownish markings around the edges of the forewings and gray veins on the underside of the wings. A hardy butterfly, it can be found from lowlands to mountains and in freezing cold to very hot temperatures. Its caterpillars, which have black and yellow stripes, feed on rock cress, jewel flower, and different types of mustard plants. The species is found in the west of Canada and the United States.

Family: Pieridae
Wingspan: 1¼–1½ in (3–4 cm)
Flight period: One, from February to July

Western White
(Pontia occidentalis)

This butterfly has black-and-white checkered wings with olive-green scales on the underside of the hindwings. Females have more markings than the males. The western white lives around lowlands such as clearings and fields, but also lives in mountainous regions in the arctic. Caterpillars are green with light and dark bands. The species is found in Alaska, and in the west of Canada and the United States.

Family: Pieridae
Wingspan: 1¼–1¾ in (3–4.5 cm)
Flight period: One or two, from April to September

Checkered White
(Pontia protodice)

Against a white background, this butterfly has dark checkering that gives it its name. Females have more dark marks than the males. The underside of the hindwings is an olive-green color. The checkered white lives around lowland open spaces, especially in wastelands and weedy plots. The caterpillars are blue-green with black speckles and feed on many types of mustard plants, bee plants, and capers. The species is found in southern Canada and in nearly all of the United States.

Family: Pieridae
Wingspan: 1¼–1¾ in (3–4.5 cm)
Flight period: Three or four, from March to November

Pale Crescent
(Phyciodes pallida)

This butterfly is pale orange with black lines and spots. The underside of the hindwing is yellowish with brown markings and a whitish crescent-shaped mark. This butterfly flies around foothills, valleys, canyons, and washes. Females lay their eggs on thistles and the caterpillars, which are ocher with brown stripes and spines, feed on these thistle plants. The species is found in parts of southwestern Canada and in the western United States.

Family: Nymphalidae
Wingspan: 1¼–1¾ in (3–4.5 cm)
Flight period: One, from April to June

Desert Swallowtail
(Papilio polyxenes coloro)

The patterns on this type of butterfly vary a lot, but many desert swallowtails have yellow bands or spots across black wings. They also have blue patches on the hindwings and orange eyespots. Desert swallowtails are fussy about where they live, so you will only spot them around desert washes and canyons. As no other swallowtails fly in these areas, this is a better way to identify them than color or pattern. The caterpillars, ringed with green, cream, and black, like to feed on Queen Anne's lace and other plants of the carrot family. The species is found in the southwestern United States.

Family: Papilionidae—Wingspan: About 2¾ in (7 cm)
Flight period: All year round, but most common in early spring

Rocky Mountain Skipper
(Polites draco)

The male of this butterfly is dark brown with a big orange patch and a large black mark on its forewings. Females are bigger and are mostly dark brown with a row of yellow marks on both wings. The underside of the wings of males and females is the same olive or greenish-gray, and there are yellow spots on the hindwings. Also known as the draco skipper, this butterfly lives in mountain meadows and lowlands. It is found in the Rocky Mountain region of Canada and the United States.

Family: Hesperiidae
Wingspan: About 1 in (2.5 cm)
Flight period: One, from June to August

Northern Blue
(Lycaeides idas)

Males and females of this butterfly look completely different from one another. Males have bright blue wings with a narrow dark border, but females have gray-brown wings with rows of orange spots around the margins. The underside of the wings is dirty-white, with a black line around the margins, orange spots inside this line, and scatterings of black spots on the rest of the wings. Look for the northern blue in mountains, heaths, bogs, and clearings. The caterpillars feed on lupines, crowberry, laurel, and Hudson Bay tea. The species is found from Alaska, through most of Canada, and into the far northern regions of the United States.

Family: Lycaenidae
Wingspan: 1–1¼ in (2.5–3 cm)
Flight period: One, from June to August

Keeping Records

You might want to keep a diary recording when and where you found your butterflies. Always take your field notebook with you when you go butterfly hunting. Make sketches of the area and the butterflies you see for your diary, or take photographs.

Butterfly diary

Keep your diary on separate sheets of paper held in a loose-leaf binder. Fill out a sheet for each butterfly-hunting trip you go on with the details from your field notebook.

You can also write notes in it when you visit museums or see a television program about butterflies. You can decorate the diary with your own drawings, photographs, pictures from magazines, postcards, and so on.

Butterfly walk

A good way to find out about butterflies in your neighborhood is by making a regular "butterfly walk." This is how to do it:

1 **Plan a route that takes about one hour to walk** (about 2 miles [3.2 kilometers]). Make sure it takes you past the different habitats in your neighborhood (like fields, woods, lakes, parks, etc).

2 **Try to take this walk once a week** during the warmest time of the day. Try not to take your walk when the weather is wet or windy.
3 **Take your field notebook and this guidebook with you.**
4 **Record each butterfly** that comes within 15 feet (4.6 meters) of you.

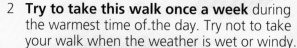

Keeping a record

You can also record each species of butterfly that you see in a card index. The file should have a card for each species that gives detailed information like:

- the butterfly's common name, its scientific (Latin) name, and the family to which it belongs
- the date on which you saw it
- where you saw it—with the name and a description of the place
- the type of habitat it is
- the weather on the day of your visit

You may be able to store your information on a computer. Keep an up-to-date printout as well as a disk.

5 **Record your weekly information in a separate part of your butterfly diary.** Over the weeks, you will see which areas are best for butterflies and which species are most common at what time of year. Does your local pattern match the flight-time information in this book?

Make a butterfly kite

Butterflies are so beautiful, they have inspired artists for centuries. Long ago, kite-makers in China made butterfly kites to flutter in the wind. You can make your own butterfly kite with some strong paper, two straws, some thin string, Scotch tape, and paints or markers.

1 **Draw an outline of a butterfly on a piece of paper.** Color in the wings with your paints or markers, giving them whatever pattern you like.
2 **When dry, cut the shape out from the paper,** being careful to keep the paper in one piece.
3 **Make some antennae from the string** and glue them to the butterfly's head.
4 **Place a long piece of string against the body of the butterfly.** Lay the straws diagonally across the wings, on top of the string.
5 **Tape the straws down firmly** on each of the four wing tips.
6 **Tie the string and the straws together** over the middle of the butterfly. Now your kite is ready to fly!

Woodlands & Clearings

The woodland habitat includes two different types of woods. Deciduous, broadleaf forests are made up of trees that lose their leaves in winter, such as oak, beech, and ash. These trees have broad, flat leaves. Coniferous forests are green all year round and include pines, firs, spruce, and redwoods. These trees have needlelike leaves.

Coniferous forests, which occur mostly in the west and north of Canada and the United States, have few flowers growing on their floors because the trees there let in so little sunshine. But some butterflies, such as the pine white, like to feed on pine needles, so this lack of flowers does not matter.

Deciduous woodlands and forests are more common in the central and eastern regions. There the bare trees let in plenty of light during the springtime, which allows lots of wild flowers to grow on the forest floor. Here, you'll find butterflies drinking nectar, or resting on twigs and branches in sunny clearings (gaps among the trees). Don't forget to look for caterpillars feeding on leaves and plants.

Clearings are found in both types of forest. The gap in the forest roof lets in sunlight and fast-growing plants take advantage of this before the slower-growing saplings shoot up to fill the hole. This picture shows butterflies from this section—how many can you recognize?

Clockwise, from the top left corner: dun sedge skipper, rambling orange, blue mistletoe hairstreak, goatweed butterfly, eastern pine elfin, silvery blue, silver-spotted skipper, and the pine white at the center right of the picture.

Great Purple Hairstreak
(Atlides halesus)

This butterfly is also known as the great blue hairstreak. Males of this butterfly have brilliant, iridescent blue wings with a dark margin and green marks on the forewings. Females are a less bright blue. Both males and females have two tails on the ends of their hindwings, one long and one short. The underside of their wings is purplish-gray. Its green caterpillars feed on the mistletoe that grows on trees such as oaks, walnuts, and sycamores. The species is found in the southeastern and southwestern United States.

Family: Lycaenidae
Wingspan: 1¼–1½ in (3–4 cm)
Flight period: Two, from
February to April, and
from July to October

Silvery Blue
(Glaucopsyche lygdamus)

The name of this butterfly applies to the male, which has silvery-blue wings with dark margins. Females have brown wings with only a little blue on them. On the underside of the wings, males and females are the same pale gray with black spots. The silvery blue does not fly very fast. It appears in early spring in woodlands, meadows, and canyons. The caterpillars' favorite plants include deerweed, lupine, wild pea, vetch, and locoweed. The species is found in most of Canada and in the northern and western United States.

Family: Lycaenidae
Wingspan: 1–1¼ in (2.5–3 cm)
Flight period: One,
from March to July

Blue Mistletoe Hairstreak
(Callophrys spinetorum)

This butterfly is also called the thicket hairstreak, because it likes to fly around thickets and woodlands, sipping nectar from flowers. It has blue-gray wings, which are slightly brighter in the males. The underside of the wings is reddish-brown with a black-edged white line that makes a "W" shape on the hindwing. The "mistletoe" name comes from its caterpillars' favorite food, which they eat off pine, fir, and juniper trees. The species is found in the west of Canada and of the United States.

Family: Lycaenidae
Wingspan: 1–1¼ in (2.5–3 cm)
Flight period: One or two,
from March to September

Western Tailed Blue
(Everes amyntula)

As its name suggests, this butterfly has a tiny, thin tail on each hindwing. Males have lavender-blue wings with a narrow, dark margin. Female wings are brown with blue on them, and orange spots at the bottom of the hindwings. The underside of the wings of both males and females is white, with dark spots and a faint orange mark on each hindwing. The western tailed blue flies in moist meadows, waysides, on roadsides, and in clearings. Plants that its caterpillars feed on include locoweed, peas, and vetch. The species is found in Alaska, western and central Canada, and the western United States.

Family: Lycaenidae
Wingspan: 1–1¼ in (2.5–3 cm)
Flight period: Two,
from spring to fall

Bramble Green Hairstreak

(Callophrys dumetorum)

Also known as the coastal green hairstreak, this small butterfly's dark gray-brown wings have no pattern. Underneath, the wings are green, with some white dashes. It can be spotted flying around evergreen forests near oceans, wastelands, chaparral, and canyons, especially in the spring. Its caterpillars are bright green or red with yellow and white lines and feed mainly on deerweed and California buckwheat. The species is found on the coast of California.

Family: Lycaenidae
Wingspan: 1–1¼ in (2.5–3 cm)
Flight period: One, from April to May

Brown Dusky Wing

(Erynnis horatius)

Also known as Horace's dusky wing, the males of this butterfly are very dark brown and females are lighter brown. Both males and females have patterns, mostly on their forewings. The forewings also feature glassy white spots and brown fringes. It flies in clearings, along woodland edges, in waste areas, and in open grassy areas. Its caterpillars feed on many different types of oaks. The species is found mainly in the eastern United States.

Family: Hesperiidae—Wingspan: 1¼–1¾ in (3–4.5 cm)
Flight period: Two to three, from January to October

Eastern Oak Dusky Wing

(Erynnis juvenalis)

Also known as Juvenal's dusky wing, this butterfly's forewings are patterned with zigzag black and light brown marks and tiny white marks near the tips. The hindwings are less patterned, with just a few mottled brown markings. A fringe runs all around the outside of the wings. You'll find this butterfly in oak woodlands, basking in the sun with its wings spread out. The caterpillars feed on various types of oak. The species is found in southern Canada and in the United States, mainly east of the Mississippi River.

Family: Hesperiidae
Wingspan: 1¼–1¾ in (3–4.5 cm)
Flight period: One or two, from April to September

Banded Oak Dusky Wing

(Erynnis brizo)

This butterfly is also called the sleepy dusky wing. With its gray forewings and contrasting brown hindwings, this butterfly is two-toned. The forewings are well patterned with black wavy lines and some white spots. The hindwings have some rows of light brown spots. A brown fringe extends around the wings. You may spot this butterfly in oak woodlands or foothills. Its caterpillars feed on several different types of oaks (and sometimes on American chestnut). The species is found in the eastern and southwestern United States.

Family: Hesperiidae
Wingspan: 1¼–1¾ in (3–4.5 cm)
Flight period: One, from March to May

Northern Pearly Eye
(Enodia anthedon)

This light brown butterfly has dark eyespots that run in a line down its forewings. Each hindwing has five eyespots that curve around, following the shape of the wing. The northern pearly eye likes shade, and you will find it in woodland clearings and waysides. It feeds on tree sap rather than flower nectar. The caterpillar is green with red-tipped horns and feeds on grasses. The species is found in most of southern Canada and the United States, except in the far western regions.

Family: Nymphalidae—Wingspan: 1½–2 in (4–5 cm)
Flight period: One or two, from June to September

Roadside Skipper
(Amblyscirtes vialis)

This small, black butterfly is also called the little black skipper. It has tiny white marks at the top of each forewing, and the margins all around the edges of the wings are checkered. The underside of the wings is brown and gray. This butterfly likes to fly around roadsides, as well as clearings, glades, and other grassy areas. Its caterpillars feed on grasses. The species is found across southern Canada and in most of the United States except for the Southwest.

Family: Hesperiidae
Wingspan: About 1 in (2.5 cm)
Flight period: One or two, from March to September

Large Marble
(Euchloe ausonides)

The wings of this butterfly, with their creamy color and mottled markings, look a bit like marble, and it is also known as the creamy marblewing. The underside of the hindwings features a green marbled effect. Look for the large marble flying low and fast around clearings, meadows, and lowlands. Its caterpillars are dark green and feed on buds, flowers, and some types of mustard plants. The species is found from Alaska through the west and central regions of Canada and the United States.

Family: Pieridae
Wingspan: 1½–1¾ in (4–4.5 cm)
Flight period: One to two, from February to August

Sharp-veined White
(Pieris napi)

Also called the mustard white, this butterfly is white with black spots and clearly visible veins. The underside of the hindwings is creamy-yellow, with clear dark scales. You can see the sharp-veined white flying along waysides and in clearings and damp meadows. Its caterpillars are green with dark or yellow stripes. They feed on different kinds of mustard plants. The species is found in Alaska, most of Canada, and the western and northeastern United States.

Family: Pieridae—Wingspan: 1½–1¾ in (4–4.5 cm)
Flight period: Two to three, from April to August

Hackberry Emperor

(Asterocampa celtis)

This butterfly gets its name from the hackberry leaves that its caterpillars eat. The butterfly has a busy pattern of black, white, brown, and gray markings on its wings. The undersides of the wings are gray-blue and patterned. Look for this butterfly around hackberry trees in woodlands or along trails. The species is found in the United States in the central and southern regions.

Family: Nymphalidae
Wingspan: 1¾–2¼ in (4.5–5.75 cm)
Flight period: Three, from March to October

Dogface Butterfly

(Zerene cesonia)

Look closely at the forewing of the male of this butterfly. Can you see a poodle's head at the edge of the black margin? The black spot looks like its eye. Females do not have such a thick, black margin on the edge of their wings. A yellow butterfly, the dogface has an orangey color on its underside. This butterfly lives around open woodlands, scrub, and desert. Its caterpillars are often green and feed on several plants, including clovers. The species is found in the United States from southern California to Florida, but it also migrates north to the northeast and Great Lakes.

Family: Pieridae
Wingspan: 2–2½ in (5–6.5 cm)
Flight period: Continuous in the South; from June to August elsewhere

Pine White

(Neophasia menapia)

The male of this butterfly has a white background, with black tips on the forewing and gray veins on the hindwing. Females have a quite different yellow background, with orange margins on the hindwings. You will find the pine white in pine and fir forests, fluttering high among the trees. Sometimes they flutter down to take nectar from flowers on the forest floor. Their caterpillars are dark green with white stripes and feed at the bottom of pines and firs. The species is found in southwestern Canada and most of the western United States.

Family: Pieridae
Wingspan: 1¾–2 in (4.5–5 cm)
Flight period: One, from July to September

Rambling Orange

(Eurema nicippe)

Orange wings with thick black borders are the hallmark of this butterfly, which is sometimes called the sleepy orange. Underneath, the male's wings are pale yellow with brown blotches and the female's wings are orange and brown. Look for this insect flying rapidly in the summertime around fields, woodlands, and mountain canyons. Its caterpillars are thin and green with white, yellow, and black stripes. Their favorite foods include senna and clover. The species is found through the southern United States and as far north as the Great Lakes region.

Family: Pieridae
Wingspan: 1½–2 in (4–5 cm)
Flight period: Many, from March to November in the North, all months in the South

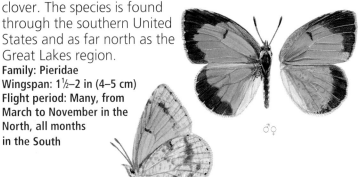

Aphrodite Fritillary
(Speyeria aphrodite)

This butterfly is an orange-brown color with black dashes and spots. The underside of the hindwings has white spots. Females of this type of butterfly are larger than the males. Look for crowds of these butterflies gathering to drink nectar from thistles—and many other flowers—around woodlands and wet meadows. They also like dry brushland, open woods, and prairies. The caterpillars, brown and spiny, feed on violets. The species is found in southern Canada and the northern United States from the Rocky Mountains to the East Coast.

Family: Nymphalidae
Wingspan: 2–3 in (5–7.5 cm)
Flight period: One, from June to September

Goatweed Butterfly
(Anaea andria)

The male goatweed butterfly has bright orange wings, and the female is a duller orange with brown marks. On the underside of the wings, both males and females are purplish-brown or gray, with brown marks. Look for the pointed tips on the forewings and the tails on the hindwings. This butterfly lives around waysides, woodlands, and streams. Its caterpillars, which are greenish with bumps and horns, feed on goatweed. The species is found in the Midwest, South, and Southwest of the United States.

Family: Nymphalidae
Wingspan: 2½–3 in (6.5–7.5 cm)
Flight period: Many, from March to November

Harvester
(Feniseca tarquinius)

The harvester is easy to spot with its orange color and brown borders and markings. It flies slowly around its damp woodland habitat visiting twigs and leaves instead of flowers. There is a pattern of dots and grayish circular markings on the underside of the wings. The caterpillars, which are greenish-brown in color, are unusual because they are carnivores. Instead of plants, they eat wooly aphids, a type of insect that lives on trees and bushes. This butterfly is found in the eastern half of the United States and southern Canada.

Family: Lycaenidae
Wingspan: 1¼–1¾ in (3–4.5 cm)
Flight period: Two in the North; continuous in the South, from February to December

Comma Anglewing
(Polygonia comma)

A ragged outline and a sharp division between forewings and hindwings are distinguishing traits of this butterfly. Its wings are a reddish-brown color with black blotches and a row of yellow spots near the dark margin on each side. On the underside of the wing is the reason for its name—a silver "comma" mark against a background of dark brown. Look for the comma anglewing darting about in clearings and waysides. Its caterpillars, light green and spiny, feed on hops and nettles. The species is found in the central and eastern regions of the United States and in southern Canada.

Family: Nymphalidae
Wingspan: 1¾–2 in (4.5–5 cm)
Flight period: Three, from March to October

Question Mark
(Polygonia interrogationis)

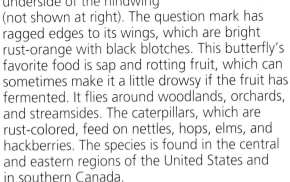

This butterfly's unusual name comes from the silver mark in the shape of a question mark on the underside of the hindwing (not shown at right). The question mark has ragged edges to its wings, which are bright rust-orange with black blotches. This butterfly's favorite food is sap and rotting fruit, which can sometimes make it a little drowsy if the fruit has fermented. It flies around woodlands, orchards, and streamsides. The caterpillars, which are rust-colored, feed on nettles, hops, elms, and hackberries. The species is found in the central and eastern regions of the United States and in southern Canada.

Family: Nymphalidae
Wingspan: 2½–2¾ in (6.5–7 cm)
Flight period: Two to five, from May to September

Comma Tortoise Shell
(Nymphalis vau-album)

Also called the Compton tortoise shell, this butterfly has wide, ragged-edged wings that are orange with black-and-white marks at the top, and a rich, rust-brown color at the bottom. Underneath, the wings are gray-brown, with a silver comma or "V" shape on the hindwing. You may see this butterfly in clearings, or by waysides or streamsides, feeding on fallen fruit or sap. The caterpillars, pale green with black spines, feed on birches, willows, and poplars. The species is found in much of Canada and in the United States, except in the far South.

Family: Nymphalidae
Wingspan: 2½–3 in (6.5–7.5 cm)
Flight period: One, in July

Brown Broken Dash
(Wallengrenia egeremet)

Also known as the northern broken dash, this butterfly is a warm brown color with light markings. Males of this butterfly have a dark dash on their forewings, which is broken in two. The underside of the wings is similar to the top side, except there is a pale crescent of yellow on the hindwings. The brown dash flies in wet woodlands, clearings, and fields. Its caterpillars feed on panic grass. The species is found in the eastern United States, to just west of the Mississippi river.

Family: Hesperiidae
Wingspan: 1–1¼ in (2.5–3 cm)
Flight period: One, from May to September ♀

Mottled Dusky Wing
(Erynnis martialis)

This small butterfly's wings are mottled brown, as its name suggests. There are strong light and dark patches on the wings that almost look like bands. On the forewings, there are tiny white spots. The mottled dusky wing lives in woodland areas and clearings. Its caterpillars, which are light green with white specks, feed on red rood in the east and on buckbrush in Colorado. The species is found on the Great Plains and in the eastern United States.

Family: Hesperiidae
Wingspan: 1–1½ in (2.5–4 cm)
Flight period: Two, from May to July

♂♀

♂

Cobweb Little Skipper
(Amblyscirtes aesculapius)

♂♀

A dark gray-brown above and below, this butterfly gets its name from the network of "cobwebs" underneath the hindwing. The forewings have a line of white marks running across them. This butterfly, also known as the lace-winged roadside skipper, lives in wet woodlands. The species is found in the southeastern United States.

Family: Hesperiidae
Wingspan: 1–1¼ in (2.5–3 cm)
Flight period: One in the North, from January to September; many in the South

Indigo Dusky Wing
(Erynnis baptisiae)

♂♀ ♂

Also called the wild indigo dusky wing, this butterfly's wings are dark brown and rounded. The forewings are patterned with light and dark markings and also have some glassy spots near the tips. A brown fringe runs along the outside of the wings. This butterfly's name comes from the plant that its caterpillars eat, and the butterfly can be seen along waysides and woodland edges, wherever wild indigo grows. The species is found in the eastern Great Plains and east of the Mississippi River.

Family: Hesperiidae
Wingspan: 1¼–1¾ in (3–4.5 cm)
Flight period: Several, from April to September

Dusted Skipper
(Atrytonopsis hianna)

This butterfly has pointed, dark brown wings. There are several white spots on the forewings, both above and on the underside. The underside of the wings also features a violet tinge of color toward the edge. You can see the dusted skipper in open fields, woodlands, and prairies, where it drinks nectar from blackberries, strawberries, and clover. Its caterpillars feed on beard-grass. The species is found mainly in the central and eastern regions of the United States and southern Canada.

Family: Hesperiidae
Wingspan: 1¼–1½ in (3–4 cm)
Flight period: Two in the Southeast, from March to April and in October; one in the North and West, from May to June

Silver-spotted Skipper
(Epargyreus clarus)

The wings of this butterfly are rich brown, with orange marks on the forewing in the male, and similar marks in pale yellow in the female. The underside of the hindwing has a large silver spot that gives the butterfly its name. Fringes on the edges of the wings are checkered. The silver-spotted skipper can be seen in clearings, prairies, and canyons, but it also ventures into city parks and suburbs. Its caterpillars, which are light yellow-green, feed on such plants as wisteria, beggar's tick, beans, and licorice. The species is found in most of the United States and southern Canada.

Family: Hesperiidae
Wingspan: 1¾–2½ in (4.5–6.5 cm)
Flight period: One, from May to December

Western Skipper
(Ochlodes sylvanoides)

This butterfly is also known as the woodland skipper because of its preferred habitat. Both males and females have orange-and-black forewings. Males have tawny hindwings; hindwings of females are mostly brown. There are many different-looking versions of this butterfly, so it may be hard to identify. Look in woodlands, scrublands, roadsides, and waysides, where it may be sipping nectar from daisies. Its caterpillars feed on grasses. The species is found in the western United States and southwestern Canada.

Family: Hesperiidae
Wingspan: ¾–1¼ in (2–3 cm)
Flight period: One, from June to October

Cobweb Skipper
(Hesperia metea)

The wings of this butterfly are stubby and dark brown. There are orange marks on the male's forewings, and white marks on those of the female. The underside of the wings is olive-gray with a weblike pattern of white veins, which gives the butterfly its name. Look for this skipper in fields, clearings, and grassy waysides. Its caterpillars, brown with a greenish stripe down the back, feed on bluestem beard-grass. The species is found in most of the eastern United States.

Family: Hesperiidae
Wingspan: 1–1½ in (2.5–4 cm)
Flight period: One, from March to April

Arizona Powdered Skipper
(Systasea zampa)

An attractive pattern of light brown and tan marks covers the wing of this butterfly. There are white marks on the forewings, and the edge of the hindwings has wavy edges. The underside of the wings looks similar. This butterfly flies in open woody areas and desert canyons and oases. It is found in the far southwestern United States.
Family: Hesperiidae—Wingspan: 1–1½ in (2.5–4 cm)
Flight period: Several, from April to October

Southern Snout Butterfly
(Libytheana carinenta)

This big butterfly can be recognized by its dented forewing shape, by its color—which is brown with white and orange marks—and by its big "snout" mouthparts. The underside of the forewings is orange at the base, and the hindwings are pale sandy-brown. The southern snout lives in canyons and woodland areas. The species is found in all of the Southern States of the United States, and it migrates north, as far as the Great Lakes.
Family: Nymphalidae
Wingspan: 1¾–2 in (4.5–5 cm)
Flight period: Continuous in the South

Nevada Skipper
(Hesperia nevada)

Also called the montane skipper, this butterfly has orange-and-brown wings. The forewings are orange at the base, and there are orange spots against a brown background on the hindwings. A brown margin runs around the wings. You can recognize males by the black mark on their forewing. The underside of the hindwing is greenish-gray with white marks. The Nevada skipper flies in clearings, grassy waysides, and high meadows. Its caterpillars feed on grasses. The species is found in mountainous areas of southwestern Canada and the western United States.
Family: Hesperiidae
Wingspan: 1–1½ in (2.5–4 cm)
Flight period: One, from May to July

Dun Sedge Skipper
(Euphyes vestris)

Also known as the sedge witch skipper, this butterfly is easily identified, as it is pure brown with no patterns. The only markings on the wings are a black mark on the male's forewing and some tiny white spots on the female's forewing. The underside of the wings is a dull tan color. This butterfly flies in woodlands, fields, clearings, and waysides. It often lands on damp leaves. Its caterpillars, which are shiny green, eat sedges and some grasses. The species is found in much of southern Canada and the United States, except for dry regions in the West.
Family: Hesperiidae
Wingspan: 1–1¼ in (2.5–3 cm)
Flight period: One or two, from May to December

California Sister
(Adelpha bredowii)

This large butterfly has white bands running down its wings, with a bright orange blob at the tip of each forewing. The rest of the wings are brown. On the underside of the wings, the pattern is completely different, with pale blue, orange, cream, and brown bands and spots. This butterfly gets the name "sister" because its colors are like that of a nun's, or sister's, habit of certain religious orders. The California sister flies in oak woods and foothills, and drinks from damp mud and fallen fruit. Its caterpillars, dark green and brushlike, feed on oaks. The species is found in the western regions of the United States.

Family: Nymphalidae—Wingspan: 3–3½ in (7.5–9 cm)
Flight period: Two, from April to October

Tawny Emperor
(Asterocampa clyton)

This butterfly is a tawny orange-brown color. Its wings are covered in darker bars and patches, including black-and-yellow spots. Females are much bigger than males, and they are a paler color. The underside of the wings is pale, with brown areas. You may see this butterfly in woodlands near hackberry trees or along waysides. The caterpillars are bright green and striped and feed on hackberry trees. The species is found in the eastern, central, and southwestern United States.

Family: Nymphalidae
Wingspan: 2–2½ in (5–6.5 cm)
Flight period: Continuous in the far South, one from June to August in the North

White Admiral
(Limenitis arthemis)

You can recognize this butterfly by the wide white bands on its black wings, and the blue-and-red markings along the borders. Look for white admirals flapping and gliding, pursuing insects around woodlands and glades. Its caterpillars are white, olive, and green, with bristles, and they feed on birches, willows, poplars, and hawthorns. The species is found from Alaska across most of Canada, and into the central, eastern, and parts of the southwestern United States.

Family: Nymphalidae
Wingspan: 3–3¼ in (7.5–8 cm)
Flight period: Two, from June to August

Western Pine Elfin
(Callophrys eryphon)

Male western pine elfins have chocolate-brown wings; the females are an orangey-brown color. Males and females have checkered margins all around the edges of their wings. The underside of the wings is patterned with zigzag marks in black, white, gray, and reddish-brown. Look for this butterfly in spruce bogs, pine forests, and canyons. You may see it perching on shrubs or sipping nectar from wild flowers. The caterpillars feed on the young shoots of pines, including lodgepole and ponderosa pine. The species is found in the western and northeastern United States and in much of Canada.

Family: Lycaenidae
Wingspan: ¾–1 in (2–2.5 cm)
Flight period: One, from May to July

Eastern Pine Elfin
(Callophrys niphon)

Males of this butterfly have dark brown wings, and females' wings are lighter with orange blotches. Both males and females have their wings outlined with a black-and-white checkered edge. Underneath, the wings are strongly patterned with black zigzag marks, as well as white and brown markings. The eastern pine elfin can be seen in pine and spruce woodlands. There, it sips nectar from wild plum, lupine, and other wild flowers. Its caterpillars, which are a transparent green with white stripes, feed on the leaves of scrub, pitch, and jack pines. The species is found in the eastern and central regions of the United States and of Canada.

Family: Lycaenidae
Wingspan: ¾–1¼ in (2–3 cm)
Flight period: One, from March to June

Woodland Elfin
(Callophrys henrici)

Also called Henry's elfin, this butterfly has very dark brown wings, especially in the male. Females may have an orangey-brown color on their wings. A good way to recognize this butterfly is by the stumpy tail at the base of the male's hindwings. This butterfly lives in woodland edges, clearings, and scrubland, where it perches on twigs. Its caterpillars feed on flowers and also eat their way through fruits such as blueberries and wild plums. The species is found mainly in the eastern half of the United States and in far southern Canada.

Family: Lycaenidae—Wingspan: 1–1¼ in (2.5–3 cm)
Flight period: One, from March to April

Carolina Satyr
(Hermeuptychia sosybius)

This dark brown butterfly may be a little difficult to identify, as it may or may not have eyespots on the top of its wings. When present, the eyespots are small. The underside of the wings has brown lines with a row of eyespots inside the margin. These eyespots have rims and are blue on the inside. This butterfly likes moist areas, shade, and grasses, so you may see it in shady woodlands and in meadows, visiting flowers. Its caterpillars, light green with dark green stripes, feed on different kinds of grasses. The species is found in the southeastern United States.

Family: Nymphalidae
Wingspan: 1¼–1¾ in (3–4.5 cm)
Flight period: Two, from April to October, in the North; continuous in the far South

Striped Hairstreak
(Satyrium liparops)

The topside of this butterfly gives no reason for its name, as the wings are plain dark brown. But the underside of the wings features three broken stripes of black, bordered with white. There are also orange and blue marks near the tails. Look for the striped hairstreak high in the trees of woodlands or within prickly hawthorn thickets. Its caterpillars are green with yellow stripes. Their foods include oaks, willows, hollies, blueberries, plums, hawthorn, and rosebushes. The species is found in much of the United States and Canada east from the Rocky Mountains.

Family: Lycaenidae
Wingspan: 1–1½ in (2.5–4 cm)
Flight period: One, from July to August

Edward's Hairstreak
(Satyrium edwardsii)

This butterfly, also called the scrub oak hairstreak, is a warm brown color both above and underneath its wings. There is a tiny tail on each hindwing. Although there is no pattern above, the underside of the wings is streaked with dark brown spots ringed with white. There are also orange markings near the margin, as well as blue spots. This butterfly likes to fly around the scrub oak thickets for which it is named. It has brownish caterpillars that feed on oaks. The species is found mainly in the northeastern United States.

Family: Lycaenidae
Wingspan: 1–1¼ in (2.5–3 cm)
Flight period: One, from June to July

Red-banded Hairstreak
(Calycopis cecrops)

Males of this butterfly have dark brown wings, but females look a little different, with blue patches on their wings. The reason for the butterfly's name is obvious once you've seen the underside of the wings—across a background of light brown is a bright red band, edged with white and black. There is also a blue spot on each hindwing, near the two tails. The red-banded hairstreak flies along waysides and the margins of woodlands. Look for these butterflies just as it gets dark, as this is when they are most active. The caterpillars are pale yellow, and their favorite food includes dwarf sumac, cotton, and wax myrtle. The species is found mainly in the southeastern region of the United States.

Family: Lycaenidae
Wingspan: ¾–1 in (2–2.5 cm)
Flight period: Three, from April to October

Northern Metalmark
(Calephelis borealis)

This butterfly's wings are chestnut-brown on top and light orange underneath. There are black patterns both above and below. Shiny silvery marks run down the wings, giving it the name "metalmark." This butterfly prefers dry habitats, such as forest clearings and meadows, especially around limestone outcroppings. Its green, black-spotted, hairy caterpillars feed on ragwort. The species is found in the United States from Indiana and Kentucky east to New Jersey and Virginia.

Family: Riodinidae—Wingspan: 1–1¼ in (2.5–3 cm)
Flight period: One, from June to August

Find Out More

Glossary

abdomen: the third section of an insect's body; it carries the ovipositor

alpine meadow: high meadow found on mountains above the timberline

bog: soft, wet, spongy ground; marsh

camouflage: coloration or other disguise that allows an animal to blend in with its surroundings

caterpillar: young stage of a butterfly or moth

chrysalis: name for the inactive pupal stage in the development of a caterpillar into an adult butterfly

dimorphic: species in which the male and female don't look alike

eyespot: brightly colored or dark marking on an insect's wing that looks like a large eye

forewings: front pair of wings on an insect

glade: small open space in a forest

habitat: environment (area) that is the natural home of certain plants and animals

hindwings: back pair of wings on an insect

iridescent: displaying changing colors, like those of the rainbow

larva: early form of an insect, such as a caterpillar or grub, before it changes into an adult form

legume: plant belonging to the pea or bean family

lichen: organism that consists of an alga and a fungus living as a single unit

metamorphosis: extreme changes in form and appearance that occur in insects and certain other invertebrates (animals without backbones) while growing to maturity

nectar: sugary liquid produced by flowering plants and eaten by insects

ovipositor: egg-laying structure on the abdomen of an adult female insect

predator: carnivorous (meat-eating) animal that eats other animals

proboscis: tubular, sucking mouthpiece of certain insects

pupa: inactive stage of an insect when it changes from a wingless larva to a winged adult

sedge: plant with rows of narrow, pointed leaves; sedge is usually found in marshy land

thorax: middle section of an insect's body; the thorax is divided into three segments, each of which carries a pair of legs—the back two segments also support the wings, if they exist

wetland: area, such as a marsh or pond, that contains water during much or all of the year

Organizations

In Canada, the **Canadian Nature Federation** is a good starting point. Contact: Canadian Nature Federation, Suite 606, 1 Nicholas Street, Ottawa, Ontario K1N 7B7; (800) 267-4088. http://www.cnf.ca

Many of the preserves owned by the **Nature Conservancy** and its chapters conserve unique and threatened habitats for insects. Contact: Nature Conservancy, Suite 100, 4245 North Fairfax Drive, Arlington, Virginia 22203-1606; (800) 628-6860. http://nature.org

The **North American Butterfly Association** publishes a quarterly magazine and seeks to promote butterfly watching. Write to: North American Butterfly Association, 4 Delaware Road, Morristown, New Jersey 07960. http://www.naba.org

The **Northern Prairie Wildlife Research Center,** part of the U.S. Department of the Interior's Geological Survey, has a very useful Web site for butterfly watchers in the United States: http://www.npwrc.usgs.gov/resource/distr/lepid/bflyusa/bflyusa.htm

The **Xerces Society** is a national society for invertebrate (animals without backbones) enthusiasts. Contact: Xerces Society, 4828 SE Hawthorne Boulevard, Portland, Oregon 97215; (503) 232-6639. http://www.xerces.org

The **Young Entomologist's Society** publishes a magazine containing articles about insects that are of interest to the beginner. Write to: Young Entomologist's Society, 6907 West Grand River Avenue, Lansing, Michigan 48906-9131. http://members.aol.com/YESbugs/mainmenu.html

Index

A

abdomen, 6
Acadian hairstreak, 25
acmon blue, 10
admiral, 6, 15, 75
alfalfa butterfly, 16
alpine, 22, 36
alpine checkered skipper, 35
American apollo. *See* clodius parnassian
American copper, 48
American painted lady, 29
American swallowtail, 7, 13
anglewing, 29, 71
anise swallowtail, 11
antennae, 6
Aphrodite fritillary, 70
apollo, 6, 10
  see also clodius parnassian
arctic, 22, 36, 47
arctic blue, 44
arctic skipperling, 41
Arizona powdered skipper, 74
arrowhead skipper, 59
aspen dusky wing, 23
Atlantis fritillary, 28
azure, 7, 15

B

Baltimore, 24
banded arctic, 47
banded hairstreak, 14
banded oak dusky wing, 67
banded skipper, 39
beard-grass skipper, 47
beating tray, 31
Behr's hairstreak, 58
black-dust skipper, 51
black little skipper, 68
black swallowtail, 7, 13, 57
black-veined skipperling, 59
black-vein skipper, 46
blazing star skipper, 40
blue, 7
  desert and mountain, 61
  found almost everywhere, 10

meadow and grassland, 34, 44
  wetland, 24
  woodland and clearing, 66
blue hairstreak, 66
blue mistletoe hairstreak, 66
bog, butterflies of, 20–29
bog copper, 26
Boisduval's blue, 34
bramble green hairstreak, 67
broad marsh skipper, 27
broad-winged skipper, 27
broken dash, 72
bronze copper, 16
brown, 7, 23
brown arctic, 36
brown broken dash, 72
brown dusky wing, 67
brown elfin, 14
brown-rim skipper, 47

brush-footed butterfly, 7
buckeye, 37
butterfly
  conservation, 2
  families, 7
  information sources, 78–79
  life of, 4
  parts of, 6
butterfly watching
  equipment and methods, 18–19
  garden for, 52–53
  hunter's code, 2
  larva and pupa, 30–31
  raising butterflies for, 42–43
  record-keeping, 62–63

C

cabbage butterfly, 10
California sister, 75

Carolina satyr, 76
caterpillar, 4
  collecting, 30
  raising, 42–43
  see also specific species
checkered skipper, 13
checkered white, 60
checkerspot, 37, 48
chrysalis, 4, 30–31
cinquefoil copper, 26
clearing, forest, butterflies of, 64–77
cliff swallowtail, 57
clodius parnassian, 7, 27
clouded skipper, 6, 35
cloudless sulfur, 16
cloudy wing, 38, 44
cobweb little skipper, 72
cobweb skipper, 73
columbine dusky wing, 56
comma anglewing, 71
comma tortoise shell, 71
common alpine, 36
common banded skipper, 39
common blue, 34
common checkered skipper, 13
common hairstreak, 14
common sooty wing, 13
common sulfur, 50
common wood nymph, 37
Compton tortoise shell, 71
coniferous forest, 64
copper, 7
  found almost everywhere, 16
  meadow and grassland, 32, 35, 44, 48
  wetland, 26
coral hairstreak, 45
cranberry bog copper, 26
creamy marblewing, 68
crescent, 60
crescentspot, 49
crossline skipper, 59

D

dainty sulfur, 58
deciduous tree, 64
Delaware skipper, 46

Additional Resources

Butterflies and Moths David A. Carter (Dorling Kindersley, 2002).

Butterflies in the Garden Carol Lerner (HarperCollins, 2002).

Butterflies of North America Jim P. Brock and Kenn Kaufman (Houghton Mifflin, 2003).

The Butterflies of North America: A Natural History and Field Guide James A. Scott (Stanford, 1997).

Butterflies Through Binoculars: A Field Guide to the Butterflies of Eastern North America Jeffrey Glassberg (Oxford, 1999) and **Butterflies Through Binoculars: A Field Guide to the Butterflies of Western North America** (2001).

A Field Guide to Eastern Butterflies Paul A. Opler (Houghton Mifflin, 1998) and **A Field Guide to Western Butterflies** (1998).

National Audubon Society Field Guide to Butterflies Robert M. Pyle (Knopf, 2000).

Index

desert, butterflies of, 54–61
desert swallowtail, 61
diary, butterfly, 62
dimorphic skipper, 39, 51
dion skipper, 40
dogface butterfly, 69
dorcas copper, 26
draco skipper, 61
dreamy dusky wing, 23
dun sedge skipper, 74
dusky wing, 23, 47, 56, 67, 72
dusted skipper, 73
dwarf yellow, 58

E

eastern cloudy wing, 38
eastern oak dusky wing, 67
eastern pine elfin, 76
eastern sedge skipper, 40
eastern tailed blue, 10
Edward's hairstreak, 77
egg, of butterfly, 4
elfin, 14, 24, 69, 76
emperor, 69, 75
eufala skipper. See gray skipper
European skipperling, 46
eyed brown, 23

F

faunus anglewing, 29
field crescentspot, 49
fiery skipper, 51
fire-rim tortoise shell, 37
flame copper, 48
flower, in butterfly garden, 52–53
forest arctic, 22
forest copper, 26
Freyja's fritillary, 26
fritillary, 7
  meadow and grassland, 48, 49
  wetland, 26, 28, 29
  woodland, 70

G

garden, butterflies in, 52–53
garita skipperling, 23

giant skipper, 41, 57
giant swallowtail, 12
glassy wing, 38
goatweed butterfly, 70
golden-banded skipper, 40
goldenheaded sooty wing, 56
golden sulfur, 27
gorgone checkerspot, 48
grasshopper satyr, 44
grassland, butterflies of, 32–51
gray copper, 44
gray hairstreak, 14
gray metalmark, 56
gray skipper, 6, 13
great blue hairstreak, 66
great gray copper, 44
Great Plains checkerspot, 48
great purple hairstreak, 66
great spangled fritillary, 49
green comma, 29
green hairstreak, 67
greenish blue, 24
greenish little skipper, 7, 12
green skipper, 51
grizzled skipper, 35

H

hackberry emperor, 69
hairstreak, 7
  desert, 56, 58
  found almost everywhere, 14
  meadow and grassland, 34, 45
  wetland, 25
  woodland, 66, 67, 77
hairy dusky wing, 47
harvester, 7, 70
head, of butterfly, 6
Henry's elfin, 76
high mountain blue, 44
hoary edge, 38
hoary elfin, 24
hobomok skipper, 39
holarctic grass skipper, 39
Horace's dusky wing, 67

I

Indian skipper, 41
indigo dusky wing, 72

J

jutta arctic, 22
Juvenal's dusky wing, 67

K

kite, butterfly, 63

L

lace-winged roadside skipper, 72
large marble, 68
larva, 4
least skipperling, 41
Leonardus skipper, 40
little glassy wing, 38
little skipper, 68, 72
little sulfur, 50
little wood satyr, 6, 36
little yellow, 50
long dash, 38
long-tailed skipper, 34

M

marble, 45, 68
marblewing, 45, 68
mariposa copper, 26
meadow, butterflies of, 32–51
meadow fritillary, 48
Melissa arctic, 47
Melissa blue, 34
mesquite metalmark, 56
metalmark, 7, 14, 25, 56, 77
metamorphosis, 4
Mexican yellow, 45
Milbert's tortoise shell, 37
milkweed butterfly, 7
mistletoe hairstreak, 66
monarch, 17
Mormon metalmark, 7, 14
Morrison's silver spike, 59
moth, butterfly compared to, 53
mottled arctic, 47

mottled dusky wing, 72
mountain, butterflies of, 54–61
mourning cloak, 11
mud-pudding, 20
mustard white, 68

N

net, for butterflies, 19
Nevada skipper, 74
northern blue, 61
northern broken dash, 72
northern cloudy wing, 44
northern dimorphic skipper, 39
northern metalmark, 77
northern pearly eye, 68
northern willow hairstreak, 25

O

oak dusky wing, 67
ocellate fritillary, 29
Olympia marblewing, 45
orange, 69
orange hairstreak, 58
orange-margined blue, 34
orange sulfur, 16
orange tip, 45
ottoe skipper, 39

P

pahaska skipper, 59
painted lady, 15, 29
pale crescent, 60
pale tiger swallowtail, 25
Palmer's metalmark, 56
park, butterflies in, 8
parnassian, 7, 27
pearl crescentspot, 49
pearly eye, 23, 68
pepper and salt skipper. See greenish little skipper
Persius dusky wing, 47
pine elfin, 76
pine white, 69
pink-edged sulfur, 50
pipevine swallowtail, 11

Index

plains yucca giant skipper, 41
polixenes arctic, 47
powdered skipper, 74
prairie. See grassland, butterflies of
prairie skipper, 39
projects
  butterfly kite, 63
  butterfly safari, 18–19
  collecting caterpillars and pupae, 30–31
  raising butterflies, 42–43
  record keeping, 62–63
pupa, 4
  collecting, 30–31
purple bog fritillary, 7, 29
purple hairstreak, 66
purplish copper, 35

Q

Queen Alexandra's sulfur, 51
question mark, 71

R

rambling orange, 69
red admiral, 15
red-banded hairstreak, 77
red-disk alpine, 22
redhead sooty wing, 56
regal fritillary, 28
Riding's satyr, 44
ringlet, 46
roadside rambler, 13
Rocky Mountain skipper, 61
rosy marble, 45

S

sachem, 46
saltgrass skipper, 7, 12
sandhill skipper. See saltgrass skipper
sara orange tip, 45

satyr, 36, 44, 76
scientific names, 2
scrub oak hairstreak, 77
sedge skipper, 24
sedge witch skipper, 74
sharp-veined white, 68
short-tailed black swallowtail, 57
silver meadow fritillary, 49
silver spike, 59
silver-spotted skipper, 73
silver-studded blue, 10
silvery blue, 66
silvery checkerspot, 37
sister, 75
sketching butterflies, 19
skipper, 6, 7
  desert and mountain, 57, 59, 61, 68, 72–74
  found almost everywhere, 12, 13
  meadow and grassland, 34, 35, 39–41, 46, 47, 51
  wetland, 24, 27
skipperling, 23, 41, 46, 59
sleepy dusky wing, 67
sleepy orange, 69
small apollo, 6, 10
small copper, 32, 48
small parnassian. See small apollo
small white. See cabbage butterfly
snout, 7, 74
sooty wing, 13, 56
southern cloudy wing, 38
southern dimorphic skipper, 51
southern pearly eye, 23
southern snout, 7, 74
spicebush swallowtail, 17
spring azure, 7, 15
spring white, 60
spruce bog alpine, 22
streamside checkerspot, 37

Strecker's giant skipper, 41
striped hairstreak, 77
sulfur, 7
  desert and mountain, 58
  found almost everywhere, 16
  meadow and grassland, 45, 50, 51
  wetland, 27
sunrise skipperling, 59
swallowtail, 6, 7
  desert and mountain, 57, 58, 61
  found almost everywhere, 11–13, 17
  meadow and grassland, 36
  wetland, 25
swamp metalmark, 25
swarthy skipper, 6, 39
Sylvan hairstreak, 56

T

tailed blue, 66
tawny-edged skipper, 12
tawny emperor, 75
thicket hairstreak, 66
thorax, 6
tiger swallowtail, 17, 25, 58
tortoise shell, 37, 71
tree, butterflies in, 52, 53
two-spot sedge skipper, 24

U

ultraviolet sulfur, 51
uncas skipper, 57

V

variegated fritillary, 48
viceroy, 28

W

walk, butterfly, 62

waste ground, butterflies in, 8
western orange tip, 45
western pine elfin, 76
western skipper, 73
western skipperling, 23
western sulfur, 27
western swallowtail, 11
western tailed blue, 66
western tiger swallowtail, 58
western white, 60
western willow hairstreak, 56
wetland, butterflies of, 20–29
whirlabout, 16
white, 7, 60, 68, 69
  see also cabbage butterfly
white admiral, 6, 75
white-m hairstreak, 34
white-spot alpine, 22
white-veined skipper, 57
wild indigo dusky wing, 72
willow-bog fritillary, 26
wings, of butterfly, 6
wolf-face sulfur, 7, 45
woodland, butterflies of, 64–77
woodland elfin, 76
woodland skipper, 73
wood nymph, 37
wood satyr, 6, 36

Y

yard, butterflies in, 8
yellow, 45, 50, 58
yellow-dust skipper, 59
yellow-patch skipper, 40
yucca giant skipper, 57

Z

zebra swallowtail, 6, 36
zigzag fritillary, 26

> See *World Book's Science & Nature Guides Resources & Cumulative Index* volume for an explanation of the system used by scientists to classify living things.